BETTER THAN

Better than Working

The Glory Days of Regional Newspapers

Paul Dale

This edition published 2021 by:

Takahe Publishing Ltd.

Registered Office:

77 Earlsdon Street, Coventry CV5 6EL

ISBN 978-1-908837-19-6

TAKAHE PUBLISHING LTD.

2021

For my wife Claire, and children Megan and James

Acknowledgements

There are many people to thank for their encouragement and wise counsel during the time I spent writing this book. They include:

Bob Ainsworth, Ian Bottrill, Julie Chamberlain, Geoff Coleman, Conal O'Donnell, Len Freeman, Rob Gill, John Lamb, Dan Mason, Dave Nellist, Eleri Roberts, Iain Roxburgh, Joe Wise.

I should also thank my wife and children for urging me to keep going, and of course my publisher Steven Hodder... thanks for your help and support.

Contents

Part IV: Coventry 1986-2000

Part I

Background

Chapter One

Decline and Fall

T he next time you are on a bus or a train, look around and see how many people are reading a newspaper. I bet it won't be many. And those that are flicking through the pages will probably be reading Metro, a publication given away free each day at railway stations and in most towns and cities across Britain.

Now look to see how many passengers are staring intently at mobile phones, iPads, tablets and laptops. Some will be catching up on news, some will be playing games or listening to music, some may be paying bills or ordering goods via the internet.

Such a radical change in the way information is accessed was unthinkable when I began my career in journalism forty-five years ago. Even the most imaginative among us would have struggled to predict a world where it would be possible to find out just about anything by consulting a phone. For goodness sake, in 1975 the seemingly simple task of getting a telephone installed in your house could mean waiting several months.

The pace of technological change, the information superhighway as it was dubbed by Tony Blair in 1997, took most people by surprise, particularly the newspaper industry which does not have the greatest record for speedily embracing new ways of doing things.

When computers and word processors began to be installed in news rooms in the late 1980s, cynical news editors insisted on stockpiling typewriter ribbons and copy paper insisting that new-fangled ways of operating would never catch on. An editor of the *Coventry Evening Telegraph* famously refused to place the paper's new website address on the front page.

But the genie was well and truly out of the bottle and could not be put back. Eventually, two things begin to dawn on publishers: the core readership of their newspapers was elderly and dying off and not being replaced by new customers; younger people were no longer reading newspapers. Put these two trends together and an inescapable conclusion emerged – most of the remaining printed regional newspapers were dying on their feet.

Since 2005, more than 200 regional newspapers have closed and half of parliamentary constituencies have no daily local paper, according to research by the National Union of Journalists. As we approach the third decade of the 21st century, it is certain that a new generation of young people will copy the lifestyle of their parents who have long since felt no need to buy local newspapers. It pains me to say so, but I doubt whether a single printed regional newspaper will exist in this country by 2040 or if any do survive they will be seen in the way that we view steam engines today, a romantic anachronism symptomatic of the way things used to be in the dark ages.

All of this rapid change was way into the future in September 1975 as I entered the world of newspapers with scarcely a thought that institutions that had served local communities for maybe 200 years or more might soon be entering death row.

On the contrary, the buildings that many of these newspapers were housed in oozed confidence. The *Reading Chronicle and Berkshire Mercury*'s office may have been a dilapidated Victorian edifice but it did come with a tremendous sense of history.

The *Oxford Mail and Times*'s open-plan headquarters to the west of the city at Osney Mead, with editorial, advertising and printing all on the same floor, was purpose-built in the early 1970s and thought to be so incredibly cutting-edge that even as late as 1980 the building was a popular spot for organised tours to allow people to get a taste for themselves of the wonderful world of newspapers and to be comforted by what they must have assumed was a shiny modern future for the industry.

The *Coventry Evening Telegraph*'s fine late-1950s city centre office had a feeling of permanence about it. At its pinnacle the *Coventry Telegraph* had a daily circulation of about 130,000 and employed 600 people. Now, almost forty years after I first walked proudly through the doors as the paper's political editor, the building has been turned into a boutique hotel. Ironically, the firm developing the former *CET* headquarters developed a profitable side line by operating a tourist trail taking visitors around the remarkably well-preserved building explaining how newspapers were written and published in their glory days.

If the weight of history did not hang heavily on the shoulders of new recruits to the *Berkshire Mercury and the Reading Chronicle*, it certainly should have done. The newspapers' rambling editorial offices in Valpy Street were

4

ancient, dating back to the late 19th century, but the papers themselves boasted even more history and were among the oldest in the country.

The *Reading Mercury* was founded in 1723 and originally known as the *Weekly Entertainer*, while the *Berkshire Chronicle* first appeared in 1825. The very first edition of the *Reading Mercury* promised to publish trustworthy news, adding thoughtfully: "And when a scarcity of news happens we shall divert you with something merry."

These two weekly publications eventually became the *Berkshire Mercury and the Reading Chronicle*, mopping up along the way a number of other smaller local newspapers including the *Oxford Gazette*, the *Berkshire County Paper* and the *Newbury Herald*.

When I began work in 1975, the future of the *Berkshire Mercury* was already in doubt. In common with most other UK newspapers, the *Mercury* and the *Chronicle* had suffered a steady fall in circulation since the boom days for regional newspapers of the mid 1950s. While the *Chronicle* was thought to be safe enough, with a unique selling point of being the newspaper of record for the fast-growing town of Reading, the *Mercury* was struggling to represent Berkshire, from Windsor in the east to Newbury in the west, in any meaningful and focused way.

Reading, a town once famous for 'beer, biscuits and bulbs', had already begun a steady transformation, partly to a London commuter belt dormitory town, and also as a favoured location for new high-tech employment. The old staples – Courage's brewery, Huntley & Palmer's biscuits and Suttons Seeds – were all in the process of either moving out of town or closing, to be replaced by soulless steel and glass-fronted offices or retail parks.

The malty, hoppy, stench of the weekly brewing day wafting through the town centre, an unpleasant early morning stomach-churning experience for a young journalist suffering from the effects of too much beer the night before, would soon be a thing of the past with Courage's relocating to a site near the M4. Even the town's football club, Reading FC, stalwarts of the old third division, decided to drop the nickname *The Biscuitmen* when Huntley & Palmer's moved out, later renaming themselves *The Royals* in a hat-tip to the Royal County of Berkshire.

It began to dawn on The Reading Newspaper Company, certainly by the late 1970s, that the *Berkshire Mercury* might cease to exist, or would have to be incorporated into the *Reading Chronicle*. In the end the *Mercury* struggled on until 1987 before being put out of its misery.

My earliest days in journalism were coloured by a growing realisation among publishers that a newspaper would be forced out of business, not as you might expect if it failed to make money at all, but if it did not make the amount of profit its owners expected and sought. Nothing has happened over the course of forty-five years to change this scenario, except for a sharp increase in the demise of local newspapers thanks in part to the ready availability of free news and advertising via the internet.

To make matters worse, hundreds of independent local newspapers once in private hands, the *Reading Chronicle and Berkshire Mercury* included, were purchased by large national newspaper companies during the 1970s, 80s and 90s and the new owners' expectations of what was a reasonable profit was driven by their publicly quoted share price. By the mid 1990s, the directors of public companies typically expected newspapers to return profits upwards of thirty percent a year – an utterly impossible target. Newsrooms were stripped out, offices closed, journalists sacked and titles merged in desperate attempts to cut costs. Unsurprisingly, readers were dismayed at what was happening to their local papers and stopped buying the inferior products on offer.

The editors and publishers I worked for in the mid 1970s and early 1980s would surely have found it incomprehensible that so many publications were to disappear within the space of four decades, in some cases putting paid to 300 years of loyally serving communities with local news. They would have been nonplussed, to put it politely, at what passes now for news on the websites of many regional newspapers, from tittle-tattle about contestants on television game shows to the lurid lifestyles of so-called 'celebrities'.

For me, though, the quite extraordinary decision in 2017 by the *Birmingham Mail* to publish a list of the West Midlands' busiest 'dogging sites' – pieces of land where adults meet up for sexual activity – captured in explicit detail the sad decline of local newspapers and persuaded me to try to give a flavour of regional journalism in the 1970s and 1980s. Not only was the dogging list published, it was shamelessly repeatedly re-published via reporters' Twitter and Facebook sites with links to the original story, presumably to push up the number of 'hits' on the newspaper's social media platforms. Similar 'dogging' guides were published by other Trinity Mirror regional newspapers (the group is now called Reach) in a clear indication that tawdry clickbait of the lowest possible common denominator was deemed perfectly acceptable by editors who a few years earlier would have recoiled from treating their readers with such contempt.

The publishers of the *Reading Mercury* promised in 1723 to divert readers 'with something merry' should there be a scarcity of news. I don't suppose dogging was on their minds.

Chapter Two

Early Days

I have been inspired while writing this book by a picture on my desk of my mother and father taken in the very early 1950s. In the background is one of Britain's instantly recognisable seaside vistas, the beautiful River Camel estuary at Padstow, north Cornwall, looking in the far distance towards the sand dunes of Rock and St Enodoc golf course. The photograph depicts two people engaged to be married and clearly very much in love.

My mother, Vera Marshall as she then was, has a cheesy grin and looks like a cat that has been given a very large bowl of cream. And why not? From a rural Berkshire working-class family, she was in her early thirties with a bitter and failed wartime romance behind her while my father, Robert James Dale, was a handsome man, who by today's standards of eulogising anyone who has achieved something out of the ordinary would have been classed if not a hero then certainly as someone deserving respect as he had fought his way through every day of the Second World War and emerged physically, although certainly not mentally, unscathed at the end of the conflict.

Because he served in the Territorial Army my father was conscripted into the Royal Artillery aged nineteen following the Munich Crisis in 1938 and served through the entire war, ultimately becoming a Regimental Sergeant Major – the highest non-commissioned rank – and took part in the Allied invasion of Burma. His seven years fighting for king and country left him deaf in one ear and partially sighted in one eye, but his attempts to secure a pension for his injuries were unsuccessful with Army medics falling back on the excuse that he was not entitled to compensation because he could not prove his disabilities were the result of injuries on active service. He was not demobbed until the war in the Far East ended in August 1945 and when he returned to Padstow, the town where he was born in 1919, he along with a great many others discovered that far from receiving thanks from a grateful nation there were, as ever, precious few jobs worth having in Cornwall.

The photograph of my parents hides some dark truths. My father, although largely self-educated, was a well-read, intelligent man, who relished bellowing answers to television's *University Challenge* from his armchair and liked to polish off a cryptic crossword before tea time. Even on the day he died he left a half-finished *Daily Telegraph* puzzle behind him. But the war destroyed him mentally and although this is going to sound like a cliché, he rarely talked about his experiences fighting for king and country.

All I know of his Army career is that he was defending Plymouth with an artillery battery at Rame Head, Cornwall, at the outbreak of the war, moved to Iceland in 1940, then later on he was stationed in India and Burma. He did talk about having been to Durban and of having swum in the Red Sea, and of having had a monkey as a pet while in India. In later years he bottled his life up as his demons led him down the path of dead-end jobs, borderline alcoholism, and dependency on at least sixty Senior Service cigarettes a day. Consequently, he had to give up work at fifty-nine and was dead at sixty-nine having suffered a series of heart attacks.

My father was one of a family of seven, with two brothers and four sisters. It was a typical Cornish working-class family of the early 20th century. Sadly, I didn't know him very well until I became an adult and acquired a car which meant I could take him to various south Oxfordshire pubs and we could enjoy a beer together. He was a remote figure during much of my childhood and I saw little of him. Starting work before I woke up he would depart for the pub soon after I returned from school. Sometimes, he would stagger home from a night on the beer, the drunken rows with my mother would begin, and I'd bury my head under the pillows, fingers plugged firmly in my ears in an attempt to find some escape through sleep. On top of that, when as a child I did attempt to talk to him I found it almost impossible to understand his broad Cornish accent.

Yet, in other ways he was a kind man who kept me supplied with sweets – 'don't tell your mother' – and would often turn up outside my primary school during break-time distributing chocolate bars to me and my friends, until ordered to stop doing so by the teachers. He rarely took me anywhere, as a father might take his son, say, swimming or to the park, although occasionally as a treat he would let me accompany him to work and sit in his lorry as he toured farms and pubs.

Looking back now it is clear to me that my father, in common with many of his generation, suffered from undiagnosed post-traumatic shock disorder resulting from his wartime experiences and was almost certainly clinically depressed for most of his life.

There were rare notable exceptions, though, when he would appear cheerful and take part in normal family life. I recall early holidays at Ventnor in the Isle of Wight when, as a small boy, I would be taken by my father to feed the ducks, and on one occasion when we were staying with my aunt and uncle at Plymouth he took me to Rame Head to demonstrate where artillery guns had been positioned in 1940, and we picked wild mushrooms in the fields. I suppose the reason why these events remain vivid after so many years have passed is because they were so rare.

He relished Christmas. I think, like me, he loved the sentimentality and, perhaps, the good neighbourliness that the festive season brings. We always had a real Christmas tree (supplied free of charge by one of my Dad's mates up the pub who worked for the Forestry Commission) which would be put up a few days before Christmas Day. Ancient decorations were brought down from the loft, dusted off, and hung from the living room ceiling. On Christmas Day lunchtime my father would return from the pub and conceal half crowns in our Christmas pudding – equivalent to 25p today, or about £5 now when inflation is added on. The half crowns were carefully removed by my mother and taken away for 'cleaning'. I don't recall that they ever made their way to my pocket.

My parents moved from Cornwall a couple of years before I was born, choosing to settle near Reading, my mother's birthplace, where jobs were more plentiful. I was born on May 1 1956 at the Battle Hospital, Reading, Berkshire. It was a premature birth, I weighed not much more than a couple of pounds and was not expected to live.

This was very much a last chance pregnancy for my mother at the age of thirty-eight, dangerously old to give birth in the 1950s. Three years before I was born my mother had a pregnancy terminated at seven months at Redruth Hospital in Cornwall having been informed that high blood pressure and septicaemia meant her baby was dead. The foetus of a boy was removed from her. My brother was to have been called Peter and I often wonder what he would have been like and how different my life would have been had he lived.

My mother very occasionally talked about the baby she had lost, but only in a matter of fact way. Sometimes, however, her anger would rise to the surface: "Two nurses came up to me. They said 'you've lost the baby. We'll have to take it away.' They removed it in bits. But they could see it was a boy."

I was baptised in hospital shortly after being born with a couple of nurses standing in as godparents as the doctors believed there was little chance that I would survive. But what did they know? Some Roman Catholic friends of my mother prayed for me every day and after a few weeks and against all the odds I began to thrive and was well enough to leave hospital for my first home, a farm on the northern outskirts of Reading, where my father had taken a job as a labourer. The sole benefit of the poorly paid job was that it came with a rent-free cottage and was within walking distance of a pub, the Pack Saddle, which for better or for worse was to become a second home for my father over thirty-odd years.

We moved around for a while as my father took a succession of farm labouring jobs, before he settled down to low-paid but more stable employment at an independent dairy, a short walk away from where we lived. His undemanding role was to drive a lorry around the farms of south Oxfordshire transporting churns of milk back to the dairy's bottling plant. It was a job that suited him down to the ground, not least because he started work at about five in the morning, finishing in the early afternoon and could arrange his route to call in at various country pubs along the way.

You would recognise the type of place where I lived from the age of five until I married at twenty-six – a ubiquitous rural council housing estate miles from anywhere. My house, at Chazey Heath just off the Reading to Wallingford road, was built a few years before we arrived in 1961 to the post-war Parker-Morris standards for local authority housing. It was modern for the time with a bathroom, a coal-fired Raeburn in the kitchen which as well as being the primary source of cooking supplied plenty of hot water. There were two bedrooms and a medium-sized garden where my father had a greenhouse and grew all manner of vegetables and fruit. The garden backed on to extensive woodlands, and there was pretty much nothing between our house and Wallingford fifteen miles away but scattered villages, undulating countryside, and the start of the Chiltern Hills.

These collections of council houses, usually in blocks of about twenty or thirty, are still to be found all over the English countryside, having been built to accommodate the army of workers that were once required to service Britain's farms and small rural industries. Our tiny estate was tagged on to the edge of sprawling post-war private housing development spreading out from Reading, huge detached rural homes with gardens more than twice the size of our entire house and garden put together. A schoolfriend lived in one of these houses. His mother fought a constant battle to stop her son 'playing with the council house children', and inevitably we lost contact when he moved to a public school.

While the views were pleasant, it was not a convenient location for a family without a car since the closest shops were three miles away and the nearest bus stop for the infrequent service to Reading a mile distant. We didn't have a phone until I left school and the nearest telephone box was half a mile away.

By the time I left home to be married in 1983, South Oxfordshire District Council had undertaken very little in the manner of maintenance or improvements to the house over the course of twenty-two years, although happily collecting the rent as the property began to deteriorate badly. Wind rattled through the windows and bindweed grew through cracks in the walls and into the front room. The council turned a deaf ear to requests to do something about this, although did religiously manage to repaint the front and back doors once every few years, which I suppose was something to be grateful for.

I'd determined at an early age to own my own house, but after checking the cost of property in the local paper had no idea how on earth I would ever be able to afford to do so. My mother advised opening a building society account, which she did for me so that I could obtain a mortgage when I grew up. But what was a mortgage, and how did it work? She had no real idea and it wasn't until much later that I realised the important thing was not the capital cost of the house, which seemed impossibly high, but whether my income was large enough to comfortably meet the monthly interest repayments.

The south Oxfordshire countryside was an idyllic place for a child to be brought up. Hundreds of acres of woodland were my playground where happy days were spent building dens and cooking sausages over fires at a time when parents didn't worry if children were missing for hours, all very much an Enid Blyton meets *Swallows and Amazons* existence.

My neighbours included several one-parent families, with more than one father serving time in prison for crimes of burglary or petty violence, so I quickly discovered there were no great expectations from most of my school teachers that the children from my estate would achieve anything very much in life. I don't wish to overplay the poverty angle, other families were worse off than ours, but this book is as much about social mobility as it is about my career in journalism, setting out how thanks to determination and, yes, some lucky breaks I avoided a life of drudgery and joined the middle classes.

Britain's obsession with the class system has always fascinated me. I am happy to describe myself as hailing from working class stock, but the suggestion that I am now anything other than middle class through and through is risible. It has become fashionable for certain Labour MPs to claim still to be working class, but this is ridiculous since members of parliament benefit from substantial salaries, gold-plated pensions and the many other perks flowing from the high-standing of their office. I left my working-class upbringing behind on the day I began work as a journalist and earned a salary rather than being paid by the hour, and being an aspirational sort of person that's something I am rather proud of.

There certainly wasn't much money to go around during my childhood. In time-honoured fashion, my father collected his wages in cash each week, deducted what he wanted for beer and cigarettes, and gave the rest to my mother to cover food, heating and the rent. There were no savings to fall back on and I recall clearly the utter humiliation when from time to time my father was forced to ask his employer for an advance on his wages in order to pay an unexpected bill, something that reinforced my determination to do better and get on in life.

There were other small incidents that went unnoticed at the time, such as the roast chicken we occasionally enjoyed on a Sunday lunchtime where my mother contented herself by eating just the two wings so that there would be enough meat for my father and me and some left over to eat cold on Monday. When I was old enough to question her about this she claimed the wings were her favourite part of the chicken and she didn't care for the rest of the meat. In an effort to put meat on the table my mother hatched a cunning plan with the local butcher, exchanging milk, cream and eggs provided by my father from his workplace, in exchange for a small joint of beef or a chicken. My mother called this barter; it was in fact theft, but luckily the dairy bosses never missed a few pints of milk and tubs of cream.

There was always a danger that coal for the Raeburn and the open fire in the living room would run out during a very cold winter, with no central heating to fall back on. My mother budgeted for coal deliveries every three months and would not easily have been able to afford to top up supplies. Even on the coldest days the living room fire was not lit until late in the afternoon, and when the temperature plummeted I'd join my father on foraging exercises in the icy, snow-covered woodlands behind the house, our breath in the freezing cold pouring out like steam trains, dragging back fallen trees which we'd then saw and chop into logs to supplement the coal supplies.

My mother experienced a rudimentary education but she did possess one incredible skill – she was a whizz at mental arithmetic and could add up, subtract and divide complicated numbers in her head hardly pausing before arriving at the correct answer. By the time I started school she had taken on a part-time book-keeping job at the dairy's wages office and the family finances began to improve. She was an assiduous saver, squirreling aside any spare money which was diverted into investments offered by Mr Latham, the Pearl Assurance man, who called at the house once a month to collect contributions. The cash, I learned later, went towards with-profits policies which, at a time of galloping inflation and high interest rates, could hardly fail to provide a decent return a few years down the line.

These insurance policies, which began to mature regularly by the time I was ten, came in handy for the late 1960s travel boom and paid for cheap package deal foreign holidays enabling my mother to take me to small family-run hotels in Spain and Italy along with an aunt, uncle and cousin who lived in Plymouth. When we didn't go abroad, we went to the Isle of Wight or Cornwall and stayed in bed and breakfast establishments. My father, who declared he'd seen enough of abroad during the war, never joined us on the foreign trips although he did occasionally hire a car in my younger years and we would travel down to stay at my aunt's house in Plymouth. This meant leaving Reading in the dark hours of the early morning, which for me was an eagerly anticipated adventure made even more exciting by my role as his official cigarette holder, sitting in the front passenger seat and passing him Woodbines every ten minutes or so which he would proceed dangerously to light having taken both hands off the steering wheel to do so. But by the time I was nine or ten my father's drinking and depression took a turn for the worse and he refused to take a holiday at all for several years.

My mother's determination that I should 'get on' in life did not always work to my advantage. She ran the house along middle-class ways, or what she assumed were middle class ways. I always had a neatly-ironed linen napkin with a silver napkin ring and meals were always taken sat at the table. A table cloth was mandatory along with a salt and pepper 'cruet'. She would routinely correct my speech, ironing out the merest sign of a Berkshire or Oxfordshire accent, and when I slipped into slang she'd snap: "Ta? Ta? That's what they put on the roads. It's 'thank you, Paul'." And woe betide referring to watching the 'telly'. It was always the television in our house.

Unsurprisingly, this rigid approach to bringing up a child on a 1960s council estate was not appreciated by school friends who quickly put it about that the Dale family with their napkins, posh ways of speaking and foreign holidays were social-climbing snobs who thought they were too good for their neighbours.

I was by all accounts an opinionated and fairly obnoxious only-child; some might say nothing much has changed. A fluent speaker with an extensive vocabulary by the age of eighteen months I apparently didn't fail to tell adults what I thought of them. Precocious but definitely not a prodigy, that was me. On one deeply embarrassing occasion when I suppose I was about three my mother was walking home with me in a pushchair when coming towards her was a local dignitary, Lady Smith, the wife of Reading fire chief Sir Harry Smith. My mother, no doubt bowing and scraping, stopped to make respectful conversation. Lady Smith, it emerged, was returning from her hairdressers where she had undergone a 'blue rinse', common in those days among ladies of a certain age, leaving her hair a distinctly odd colour. This was too much for me and summoning a loud voice I declared: "I don't like your hair." Lady Smith gamely replied that she was none too keen on it either, to which I responded: "I hate your hair." My poor mother must have wished she could disappear into the nearest hole in the ground never to be seen again.

On another occasion, again in the pushchair, which quite clearly brought out the worst in me, a baker making deliveries in the area unwisely attempted to stop a tantrum by pacifying me with a cream bun, a sticky confection that I'd probably never experienced before. "Here you are, luv, this'll put a smile on his face." Showing early promise for the cricket field, I swiftly despatched the bun back, hitting him squarely in the face.

I was once marched home in disgrace from a Christmas Punch and Judy party at the home of the owner of the farm where my father worked, having shouted "It's not real, there's a man at the back with puppets."

Everyone needs a bit of luck in their lives, and as a child growing up I benefited from several pieces of good fortune. There was no public library within walking distance, but I was given a second-hand set of children's encyclopaedias that my father had acquired from one of his 'contacts' at the pub, and a natural thirst for learning meant that I had a pretty good command of general knowledge by the time I was ready for secondary school. As luck would have it, my mother's older sister lived nearby in a large detached house, having married a local government officer. They had a daughter, my cousin, who was eleven years older than me and lived a decidedly comfortable middle-class lifestyle with a car.

I spent more time with them as I grew older and there were regular picnic trips to the countryside and outings to restaurants, with the Berni Inn at Henley being a regular haunt, although for reasons of cost I was never permitted to order anything more lavish than cod and chips – the scampi had to wait until the glorious day I pocketed my first wages. Eating out widened my horizons and gave me a glimpse of a better way of life, although I knew progress in the form of buying a house and getting a decent job was only likely to be achieved through obtaining academic qualifications. By the time I was in my mid-teens my cousin often came to the rescue, taking me to her house to stay for a day or so when the rowing between my parents became too much to bear. Her kindness gave me a better chance in life, for certain.

My parents weren't interested in politics as such. They shared a cynical disregard for all governments, regarding politicians as existing simply to screw working people. But they were keen on current affairs and believed it was important to keep up with the news. My mother was a Labour voter who used to take great pleasure in being given a lift to the polling station by Conservative organisers – and then sneakily placing her cross opposite the Labour candidate in the privacy of the polling booth, a metaphorical V-sign to her driver.

I vividly recall being taken with my mother by my aunt and uncle to witness Winston Churchill's funeral cortège pass through Pangbourne railway station in 1965. The small platform was packed with those determined to pay their last respects to Britain's great wartime leader. Men stood on a bitterly cold day, heads bowed, wearing their medals, hats removed, and I recall absolute silence as the steam locomotive carrying Sir Winston's coffin roared through and on towards his final resting place at Bladon.

I gained a pretty good knowledge of national and international news even as a small child since the BBC Home Service, now Radio 4, was inevitably playing in the background on a large Bakelite radio purchased by my parents in 1953 following my mother's failed pregnancy. They'd saved money for a baby, but spent it instead on a radio which I recall had an impressive dial which could connect listeners to the likes of seemingly exotic radio stations across Europe in Paris, Nice, Berlin, Moscow, and, of course, Luxembourg. After Sunday lunch my father would doze in his armchair and listen to *The World at One* – 'sixty minutes of news and views from Britain and around the world' – followed by *Gardeners' Question Time*. *Just a Minute* with the irrepressible Kenneth Williams was another favourite as was *The Archers*, an everyday story of country folk.

I experienced pretty much every type of state school it was possible to attend in the 1960s and 1970s, starting at a small, rural Church of England primary school then moving to a sprawling Secondary Modern in 1967 at the age of eleven, which converted to comprehensive status, and then on to Henley-on-Thames Grammar School aged sixteen, which was in the process of conversion into a sixth-form college while I was there. Two of the schools stood out – the primary school for instilling discipline and a decent grounding in maths and English, and the grammar school for outstanding teaching and unrivalled facilities including an extensive 200-year-old library, a manicured cricket ground, and even a heated outdoor swimming pool.

My primary school was in many ways stuck firmly in the 1950s. I can't recall lessons consisting of anything other than grammar, spelling and maths. On special occasions, the birthday of the Queen and other members of the royal family, a radio would be wheeled into the hall at lunchtime so that children could stand and listen to the National Anthem being played on the Home Service to mark the occasion. But even then, there were clear signs that times were changing. The headmaster and his wife, Mr and Mrs Jones, who were approaching retirement age, made a show of standing to attention, heads bowed respectfully. Other younger teachers equally made a show of defiantly remaining in their seats.

This was the time of the Cuban Missile Crisis when the world came closer to nuclear annihilation than ever before or since. I don't recall the events being talked about by my mother or father, but I do remember one of my teachers warning us we shouldn't be concerned about the Soviets, the Chinese were the ones to fear because they would dominate the world by the time we were grown up, with devastating consequences for peace.

My first secondary school, a three-mile bus ride away, was a rough place when I was there. Huge fights between rival gangs were a regular occurrence on the playground, with the younger male teachers only too keen to wade in, fists flying, to sort out the hooligans. A teenager was sent home for carrying a knife and another lad ended up at the hospital casualty unit having had a large stone smashed into his head during a scrap. A boy in my class set fire to some papers in his desk during a lesson. A quick-thinking teacher swiftly opened the window, picked the desk up and hurled it outside. We never saw the arsonist again, who presumably was told to leave.

There was no sixth-form at the school which didn't really matter since the standard of teaching was pretty poor, particularly in maths and the sciences, and it was abundantly clear most of my fellow pupils weren't going to pass any O Levels let alone go on to study A Levels. The teacher responsible for imparting careers advice once asked me what type of job I would be looking for when I left school. I replied rather ambitiously that I'd like to read the television news. The teacher, scarcely disguising a sneer, replied that I'd need a very good education to secure such a job, something that even at a relatively tender age I could see was never going to be available at his school.

Some of the teachers were as borderline-psychopathic as the delinquents they were supposed to teach. One kept a heavy metal set square handy which he would whizz through the air at misbehaving pupils rather in the manner of Oddjob hurling his steel bowler hat in the James Bond film *Goldfinger*. Another sadistic teacher liked to inflict corporal punishment on boys in front of the class. His preferred method was to draw a chalk cross on the seat of the miscreant's trousers and a second cross on the slipper, attempting to line up the two crosses as he relentlessly beat his victims with a gym shoe. And of course, the hurling across the classroom of blackboard rubbers was commonplace.

My teachers didn't want to enter me for GCE O Levels, preferring instead the less academic CSEs. The problem with CSEs (Certificate of Secondary Education) was that, no matter how good the grades you were awarded, the exam did not entitle you to take A Levels. My mother was having none of this and, to her eternal credit, got on her bike and cycled to the school to remonstrate with the head. I was grudgingly permitted to sit five O Levels which I passed with some ease, including a prized Grade One in a subject called British Constitution, which was a grand title for British politics. This, then, proved to be a turning point in my young life by opening up the pathway to a decent school.

Henley-on-Thames Grammar School was founded in 1604, making it one of the country's older educational establishments. The classrooms dated from Victorian times, the school having moved from its original town-centre site in the 19th century. Although the conversion to a sixth-form college was underway when I arrived, HGS was run very much like a minor public school under strict disciplinarian headmaster David Henschel (MA Oxon). Daily morning assemblies along high church Anglican lines would be marked by Henschel's railing against modern society and denouncing a 'worrying sub-culture in this school' by which he meant students who had long hair, opposed the Vietnam War, and disagreed with his deeply-held Christian and conservative views.

Henschel was a man of such self-belief, or some might say arrogance, that he re-wrote the Lord's Prayer, assuming presumably that the original author wasn't quite up to the job. He would intone piously at assembly: "We will now say together the Lord's Prayer ... my version."

There was even a school song – "Oh Lord, keep our school forever in thy hands, stainless and bright true lore professing ever let it shine a beacon light." The more rebellious boys predictably enough sang alternative lyrics: "Oh Lord, keep my tool forever in my hand ..."

The school had a janitor and general factotum to the headmaster called Harry, who went by the glorified title of Steward. Harry, who as far as anyone knew had been there for ever, had the responsibility of ringing the school bell in the morning to mark the start of the day and ringing it again in the afternoon to signal the end of the day. Harry was definitely a man worth cultivating since one of his duties was to serve us food at lunchtime and he would often bring out extra portions of roast potatoes to favoured tables.

It is difficult to believe now, but even though HGS was in the State system prospective pupils and their parents had to attend an interview with Henschel so that the headmaster could satisfy himself that new entrants were of the right calibre to be admitted to the school. Much to the astonishment of almost everyone in my wider family, I passed the interview and was enrolled for the autumn term of 1972 – becoming only the second child on my council estate to make it to grammar school.

New arrivals at the school couldn't help but be struck by a sense of history, from the honours' boards listing scholarships and academic achievements of former students, to the book-lined library with its comfy leather armchairs and bound copies of *The Times*. Once a year we were forced to experience the eye-watering embarrassment of the annual parade of the entire school to church through the streets of Henley – pupils and teachers – to commemorate Founder's Day, an event that inevitably prompted plenty of derision and abusive comments from the local toughs who'd line the pavements and hurl insults.

In the classroom and on the school site all of the teachers wore academic gowns and you had to apply for an 'exeat' if you wanted to go to the town at lunchtime. By the time I was seventeen the exeat policy had bitten the Latin dust and was quietly dropped, allowing sixth formers free access to the town at break times. Several of us were in the habit of removing our school ties and blazers and sneaking out for a half of bitter and a game of bar billiards at the nearby A E Hobbs pub where there was an unofficial understanding that sixth-formers used the public bar and teachers frequented the lounge bar and neither recognised that the other side was there.

The A Level stream of pupils, the lower and upper-sixth, which I was in, benefited from university-style tutorials held in teachers' rooms where more informal discussions about the subjects we were studying were held. Coming from an environment where classes consisted of thirty-plus pupils in unruly chaos, most of whom weren't remotely interested in learning, this was something of an eye-opener for me and I particularly looked forward to the tutorials given by my history teacher, Steve 'Sooty' Coles, more formally known as SCC Coles, a former Oxford University, Harlequins and England scrum half, who would advise simply "dipping into" torturous volumes such as Morley's life of Gladstone rather than "reading the whole wretched thing". Grammar school also opened my eyes to intellectual pursuits such as the chess and bridge clubs and the debating society, of which I was an enthusiastic member.

My school life ceased in May 1974 after sitting A Levels. We were supposed to stay on for the rest of the term and take part in 'community activities' but I decided six weeks of playing golf and cricket would be a better plan. My mother simply told the school I'd secured a part-time job so would not be returning.

Part II

Reading 1975-1980

Chapter Three

Land of the Rising Sun

'Fancy a snifter, old boy?' Well, who was I to argue with the senior hack chosen to chaperone me on the very first day I was allowed out of the *Reading Chronicle and Berkshire Mercury* offices to report on events at the magistrates' court.

Of course, it was only 10.30 am.

Public houses and journalists go together like cheese and biscuits, and certainly that was the case in the 1970s. The first question on the lips of any newcomer to the editorial floor would not be "where's the toilet", or "where's the best place to buy sandwiches?" It would be "where's the office pub?" But even I was a little surprised, although far from downhearted, to be in the snug bar of the Rising Sun quite so early in the day.

'Mags', as the courts are routinely referred to by newspaper people, were a staple diet for weekly papers like the *Reading Chronicle and Berkshire Mercury*, where upwards of sixty pages had to be filled each week with a wide variety of stories deemed newsworthy enough to appeal to readers. Typically, the Reading courts sat every weekday and provided a rich diet of traffic offences, theft, burglary, petty crime and suchlike. They were then and remain today the starting point for serious crime – murder, arson, sexual offences – where cases would first come to the attention of newspapers before being remanded upwards to the crown court.

The magistrates began sitting at 10am, but having discovered by chatting to a friendly court usher that "there's nothing decent coming up until later" my mentor suggested that, it being a Monday and all things being considered, a swift beer or two would be very much in order. Who was I to argue? We duly left the courts and crossed over Valpy Street to the back of the *Chronicle* building where the pub door had been unlocked by the landlord a few minutes previously.

As it happened, I had only the haziest notion that public houses even opened at such a time. I wasn't much of a drinker then, although this was to change pretty rapidly. To my utter astonishment, the tiny snug bar at the back of the pub was already noisy and crowded and I instantly recognised several of the early-morning tipplers – they were my new colleagues from the reporters' room I had been introduced to an hour or so previously.

Bill Garner, the editor of the *Chronicle and Mercury* in 1975, who wouldn't have been seen dead in the Rising Sun snug, was the man who gave me my first job in journalism. He was then at the end of his career and retired a couple of years after I started. Mr Garner – you had to be very senior indeed to have dared risk calling him Bill – would have been born shortly before the First World War and possessed God-like status across the Reading Newspaper Company.

A thick-set man with slicked-back black hair, braces, and a dark, thin, pattern-less tie with a hallmark gleaming white shirt with sleeves rolled up ready for a day in the subs' room or a session in the hellish conditions of the dingy basement composing room with its foundry where our typewritten words were hammered into hot metal by a small army of sweaty compositors, Bill Garner was someone who both demanded and was afforded respect. He was a senior figure in the town's business community and, I recall, a member of the Athanaeum Club in the days when Reading had such a thing.

One of my first tasks had nothing whatsoever to do with journalism. I was entrusted to fetch Mr Garner's daily supply of cigarettes from the tobacconist around the corner. He'd give me enough cash to purchase twenty Senior Service, and meticulously count out and pocket any small amount of change when I returned. He was not a man who frittered money away on tipping junior members of staff. Nor, clearly, did he believe in paying any more for his cigarettes than was absolutely necessary.

A few months earlier, my job interview in the editor's office was memorable for being very short and distinctly understated. The room, which probably had not changed much since Charles Dickens's days, was poorly lit and made even gloomier by dark furniture. There were several leather armchairs, an ancient roll-top desk, and glass-fronted cabinets stacked with reference books and bound copies of past *Chronicle and Mercury* editions dating back 100 years or more. The only nod to the 20th century was the presence of a couple of telephones, one an outside line and the other an internal line enabling Bill to keep in contact with the subs' room, the composing room where the newspapers were printed, and the advertising and accounts offices across the road.

Bill Garner asked very little and the entire interview couldn't have lasted more than five minutes. Other colleagues at the time told similar stories of Bill's eccentric interviewing technique. Which school I had attended and bizarrely, what did my mother and father do, was about all he wanted to know. He certainly didn't come up with any of the tricky questions I had been warned to expect from college lecturers on my journalism course, such as "why do you want to go into newspapers", or "tell me a story featured on the front page of a national newspaper today", which was a pity as I had meticulously prepared the answers to both.

Bill stood up from his desk after little more than a couple of minutes, walked over to the window and stared down at the constant flow of traffic in Valpy Street below, focusing presumably on whether I might make the grade as a journalist. For what seemed an age, but was probably no more than half a minute, he said nothing at all while considering whether hiring the callow nineteen-year-old youth in front of him was a gamble worth taking. Then he turned to look directly at me.

"You'll find Reading a very newsy town. There's always something going on. Yes, there's no shortage of news, certainly."

He continued: "You'd better come back as soon as you've got your results, and we'll fit you in."

I left in something of a daze and returned home to tell my mother I wasn't entirely sure whether I'd been offered a job or not. A day or so later a letter arrived at home confirming that I would be employed as a trainee journalist at an annual salary of £880 plus 50p a week to compensate for the unsocial hours I'd be expected to work. I would be required to sign indentures providing I had successfully passed exams in shorthand, at least 100 words per minute, typing, law and public administration as set by the National Council for the Training of Journalists.

The 50p unsocial hours payment was something of a joke, even in 1975, as it came nowhere near adequately rewarding journalists for the long hours they were expected to be on call. There was no system at the *Reading Chronicle and Berkshire Mercury* for awarding staff days off to reflect time they had worked over and above the terms of their contract, or if there was no-one ever told me. If you started work at 9am and didn't finish until 10pm, that was simply written off by management as part and parcel of newspaper life and, apart from a bit of grumbling, generally accepted as the way of the world by reporters. I don't recall any of my colleagues arguing that they should have half a day off because they had worked too many hours the day before, and I'm certain they'd have been given short shrift by the news editor if they had done so.

Frugal newspaper publishers naturally turned their backs on paying overtime to journalists, thereby keeping the wage bill down and saving themselves a large amount of money. The National Union of Journalists, generally more interested at that time in supporting left-wing causes in places like Chile and Nicaragua than doing anything positive for young hacks in the provinces, didn't help by refusing point-blank to campaign for overtime payments, which were thought to be below the dignity of journalists.

It seems a lifetime away now, but in the feudal world of newspapers in the 1970s a Victorian system of indentures tied a trainee reporter to a company on a very low wage until he or she had gained a National Council for Training of Journalists proficiency certificate, and in theory someone who chose to quit or move to another paper before completing their indentures left themselves open to legal action from their former employer who could attempt to recoup the cost of training, although I'm not aware this ever happened. Once you'd gained the proficiency certificate you were classed as a senior journalist and qualified for a small pay rise.

A few months after my interview with Bill Garner, I had indeed passed the exams taken at the end of a year-long NCTJ course at Harlow Technical College. Piers Morgan, who went on to become editor of the *Daily Mirror* and is now a television presenter, was at the same college a couple of years after me although our paths never crossed.

To be frank, the course was hardly very challenging and consisted to a large extent of being entertained by the embellished stories of Fleet Street's glory days by former national newspaper hacks who were now making money on the college lecture circuit. There were regular trips to blue chip companies such as Shell, Coutts bank, and the London Stock Exchange where company chiefs were persuaded to meet "the journalist of tomorrow" and we were able to interview executives in the forlorn hope of finding a story before consuming a sumptuous boozy lunch and staggering back to Harlow.

Securing a job on a newspaper in the 1970s was every bit as difficult as it is today and the only entry point for school-leavers or graduates was to complete an NCTJ course in one of several colleges across the country, all situated in less than glamorous locations like Harlow, Preston, Cardiff and Portsmouth. There were two ways to get a foothold in journalism: either through the direct entry system by finding a newspaper prepared to take you on straight away, with block-release college courses allowing an NCTJ Proficiency Certificate to be completed three years down the road. Or the pre-entry system where you would participate in a one-year college course after completing A levels or a degree and then sit a proficiency certificate exam a couple of years later after finding a newspaper to employ you.

I've often been asked why I wanted to become a journalist, but this isn't an easy question to answer. I really had no idea as a young teenager what I wanted to do in life. It simply wasn't something I'd thought about very much, being content in my spare time to kick a football around or get on to the golf course whenever possible. While at school I'd done no homework at all for O Levels and didn't begin to do so until I had to sit A Levels. Even then, I worked as little as necessary in the evenings in order to get by. It was no secret to my family that I simply didn't get on with school. I didn't like the rules, I didn't care for the discipline. I hated the way that most teachers took the easy way out by punishing whole classes for the misbehaviour of one or two troublesome individuals. I simply wanted to leave school behind at the earliest opportunity and earn money.

In common with most post-war boys, I'd often imagined myself as a fighter pilot patrolling the skies against possible Soviet invasion. I even went as far as applying to join the RAF and was sent, just as I started at the grammar school, to a weekend assessment at Biggin Hill. It was not a great success. Having failed all of the aptitude tests, I was told the RAF wasn't for me and sent packing.

However, I'd always enjoyed English lessons and writing came easily to me, so I suppose that skill along with the somewhat romantic portrayal of journalists in Hollywood films persuaded me that this was a career that would be exciting while not involving a great deal of hard work. The truth is that in common with many of my media contemporaries, I simply drifted into newspapers while most of my friends at grammar school went on to university and ended up with careers in well-paid professions such as accountancy or the law.

The academic bar for entry into journalism in the 1970s could hardly have been set very much lower. I was informed by a somewhat relieved school careers teacher that I'd need only two A levels, any subject, any grade, to get on to the pre-entry course. The inference clearly was that even I couldn't fail, and in truth this didn't seem a very onerous task since I was taking history and geography A levels at school and two more A levels in politics and economics studying at night classes at Reading Technical College. I passed all of them much to the astonishment of my teachers and most of my family, although the grades certainly would have been higher if I'd spent less time on the golf course and cricket field and more time studying.

The obvious downside of a pre-entry course, which I completed, was that a job had to be found at the end, and the mid-1970s in three-day-week Britain beset by constant economic crises, was not a place where employment in newspapers, or anywhere else, was easy to come across, and I'd already heard plenty of horror stories from fellow students at Harlow who had been turned down for job after job.

I've never been lacking in confidence, so when I was taken on by Bill Garner it didn't seem the least bit surprising. Call it the cockiness of youth, but it's what I had expected. Only now looking back is it clear to me that I was incredibly fortunate to be accepted for an NCTJ pre-entry course, where thousands of applicants across the country fought to secure a few-hundred prized positions, and then managing to walk straight into a job in my home town setting me off on a career where every day was a great adventure and a day to look forward to. It did indeed turn out to be better than working for a living.

Chapter Four

Tea in the Subs' Room

Newspaper sub-editors are not, as some people mistakenly think, a deputy to the editor. They are in fact the glue that binds together the editorial process and their role is to check stories written by reporters, refine or rewrite if necessary, place the stories on a page and write the headlines. All trainee journalists at the *Reading Chronicle and Berkshire Mercury* were required to spend their first few weeks in the subs' room, where they could be assessed and given simple tasks such as re-writing press releases before being judged accomplished enough to be transferred to the reporters' room and let out to annoy the great Reading public. I first reported for duty in September 1975, my moped safely stowed in the Forbury Road car park, to embark on a lifetime of journalism. But I wasn't remotely prepared for the quaint eccentricity of the subs' room.

The editorial offices in Valpy Street were shoehorned into an ancient narrow building extending to four or five floors. When I arrived, the subs were all male, about six or seven in number, and were ensconced on the second floor opposite the editor's office and directly underneath the reporters' room. The top of the building was occupied by the features department, sarcastically dubbed 'cardigan corner' by fire engine-chasing reporters who regarded feature writing and the reviewing of films, plays and concerts as a cushy number for older employees.

In sharp contrast to the constant hammering on typewriter keys in the reporters' room, business in the subs' room was conducted pretty much in conditions of near funereal silence, only interrupted by the occasional tut-tutting and shaking of heads at a poorly written story, and of course the relentless stubbing out of cigarettes in multiple ash trays. A few of the subs fought a constant but doomed battle against the creeping use of clichés, slang and, worst of all, 'Americanisation' in the stories they were working on. Phrases such as 'council chiefs' instead of council officers, 'cops' instead of police, the dreaded 'mystery surrounds the death of …' opening paragraph to a story, and of course almost any use of puns were frowned upon. There was a total ban on using 'passed away' instead of 'died' and any attempt to liven up stories with descriptions such as 'an Aladdin's cave of stolen goods' would be consigned to the nearest rubbish bin.

There would be long discussions about finer newspaper style points, such as whether it would be better to write 'jail' or 'gaol' and whether assizes should really have a 'z' rather than an 's'. Goodness knows what the *Chronicle* subs would have said if faced with a story in which snow was referred to as 'the white stuff', which unfortunately seems to be commonplace on today's newspaper websites.

Some of the subs were coming to the end of their careers and had arrived in Reading after taking generous redundancy packages from Fleet Street papers. They were gently grazing and seeing out their time in the provinces. A little undemanding subbing on weekly papers in their twilight years. What was not to like about that?

There was an eccentric former Agricultural Correspondent of the *Daily Telegraph*, who occasionally took nourishment from a flask of hot milk laced with whisky. He'd amuse or bemuse everyone with pronouncements out of the blue such as: "Funny thing. The Chinese eat dogs and keep lambs as pets. We eat lambs and keep dogs as pets. Funny that."

He also kept up a lively but futile campaign against the use of the word 'mugger', then beginning to creep into English newspapers after being imported from the US, insisting that if this description was to be used at all it could only possibly apply to black men.

There was a grizzly Yorkshireman who had been a sub on the *Daily Express* and was keen to tell anyone who would listen that he had worked under that newspaper's great post-war editor Arthur Christiansen. One day, he volunteered to demonstrate to me and another new starter the art of subbing a story from the magistrates' courts. Accompanied by a sharp pencil, muttering furiously under his breath about the utter inadequacy of young reporters, he quickly reduced about twenty pieces of copy paper to four or five sheets, crossing out anything he deemed to be unnecessary or repetitious. Very quickly, a 700-word story had been slashed to about 200 words.

"Any questions lads?"

With an eye on the clock and in anticipation of rapidly approaching pub time, I ventured no opinion, but my companion, recently graduated from the

University of Oxford, with an impeccable cut-glass accent and unafraid to speak his mind, offered some laconic observations:

"Well, I couldn't help noticing, if you don't mind Sir, that you've removed all of the defence evidence and left in all of the prosecution evidence. Surely that can't be right?"

Cue mini-explosion from angry Yorkshire sub along the lines of "are you telling me how to do my job" and "he wouldn't be in court if he wasn't guilty".

While the average age of the subs' room was probably late 50s, there was one occupant who appeared to be mid-20s. He left abruptly one day after a few successes on the horses, vowing to make his fortune as a professional gambler. He was never heard of again, but the locked drawer of his desk was finally opened, to reveal a collection of rotting bread rolls apparently supplied to him each morning by his landlady, which explained the strange smell.

Another curiosity: the picture editor at the *Chronicle and Mercury* had never been a photographer. He'd been in the dim and distant past a court reporter, reputedly with astonishing shorthand at 140 words a minute, but had no experience of photography apart from taking holiday snaps. No one could quite work out how he'd been promoted to picture editor since he appeared to lack any of the qualifications necessary for the job.

The chief sub, meanwhile, had a profitable side-line in selling greyhound racing tips to the likes of *Sporting Life* and racing pages of the national newspapers. Every so often during the day he'd light a cigarette, pick up the phone, and spend fifteen minutes or so reading through a list of fancied dogs for the next day's races. When away on leave, he'd depute the picture editor to make the calls. Whether the picture editor knew any more about greyhounds than photography was a matter for debate.

One of my first duties as effectively the office junior was to field phone calls from angry readers, of which there were quite a few. Anyone calling to complain about something in that week's newspapers, usually on a Monday morning, would be put through to the chief sub who would deal with the matter courteously if he felt the complaint was justified. However, as anyone who has ever worked on the editorial side of newspapers will affirm, there were regular complainers who liked nothing better than the sound of their own voice. One such for the *Reading Chronicle* was a local vicar who would rant down the line non-stop for twenty minutes or so about the prejudices and iniquities of newspapers. My heart sank when I heard the chief sub say "Just a minute, Sir, I'll pass you over to one of my colleagues who will be able to answer your points." The only requirement from me thereafter was to mutter 'yes' and 'no' and 'quite so' at appropriate moments as the vicar worked himself up to the pinnacle of his tirade against the media, while my colleagues chuckled away contentedly while getting on with their subbing duties.

Each sub had responsibility for overseeing a number of pages in the various newspapers we produced and in the days of 'hot metal' had to make regular trips to the composing room to inspect the layout of typeset pages before signing them off for printing. But there was one big complication – the typeface had to be back to front so it would appear the right way around when printed on to paper. The best subs had the knack of being able to read the back-to-front type, while others risked the derision of printers by using a small mirror to read the words, something regarded as very poor practice in the comp room.

Every afternoon at about a quarter to four, without fail, the subs would stop working to take tea. Regardless of deadlines or the hot scoops sitting on their desks, irrespective of any huge newsworthy event unravelling in Reading and Berkshire, or indeed the world, the chief sub would declare: "Gentlemen, it is time for tea, I think."

Pens were laid down. Work would cease. The kettle would be boiled and there would then follow twenty minutes of supremely awkward Britishness. Polite chit chat over tea and cakes. No one needed to be told that politics and religion and any matters of controversy were to be avoided at all costs. That was a given and understood. Favoured topics of conversation ranged around gentle subjects such as how best to grow dahlias and the health-giving benefits of caravan holidays in Cornwall.

I was considered competent enough after a couple of weeks to go upstairs to the reporters' room where my career in newspapers would begin in earnest. Or quite possibly, the subs had simply tired of the presence of a cocky nineteen-year-old in their room and sent me packing.

Chapter Five

A Reporter at Last

The reporters' room was the same size as the subs' room, but had to accommodate more people. Anyone opening the door would be greeted by the sight of up to a dozen hacks crammed into a space where, perhaps, six or seven desks were the maximum number that could have been accommodated with ease. Notepads and pens were handed out by Mrs Graves, the editor's secretary, but when you asked for a replacement if she was in a bad mood she'd sometimes demand you produce the filled notepad, with both sides of the paper used, or prove that the pen really had run out of ink and that you hadn't simply mislaid company property.

The subs', incidentally, weren't the only eccentrics on the paper. The former chief reporter, who left just before I started, was a young man who hailed from one of Berkshire's horse-breeding families, which may be how he got the job. He was given a company mini which he proceeded to race around the county's narrow lanes until, finally, a red light came on and would not disappear. Knowing nothing about cars, or about anything else much, the hapless driver asked his colleagues about the light, and was told he'd need to top the engine up with oil. Off he went to do so, and returned about 40 minutes later with his hands, shirt and jacket sleeves drenched in sticky black oil. It transpired he'd been attempting to pour the liquid into the tiny hole for the dipstick, with predictably disastrous results.

During much of the day most of the reporters were out of the office covering courts or council meetings or attending the daily police and fire services press briefings. The very first job of the day was police calls and fire and ambulance calls. As strange as it may seem to today's journalists, it was common practice forty years ago for the local police chief inspector or superintendent to invite newspaper reporters to attend a daily briefing, usually about 9am, where any serious crimes committed or newsworthy incidents that had occurred during the previous 24 hours would be revealed over a cup of tea and biscuits, and questions could be asked by the journalists. Similar briefings took place at the fire station and ambulance station.

Towards the end of the 1970s and into the 1980s, police forces and fire and ambulance services replaced these friendly briefings with remote and sometimes less than helpful press officers who became the first point of contact for journalists via telephone rather than face to face meetings. All too often the default position of police press officers, in particular, appeared to me to be to stop information making its way to newspapers, which led to difficulties and huge frustration for journalists. The advantage of the daily press briefing was that it enabled senior police and fire officers to get to know and trust local journalists and good working relationships were formed as a result, to the obvious benefits of both sides. Press offices were more remote, defensive, and time-consuming for reporters, and paradoxically because they were intent on preventing information from getting into the public domain often ended up allowing police and fire services to be portrayed in a less than favourable light.

As deadlines approached for publication of the two weekly papers and their various district editions the reporters' room would be full to bursting with a deafening clattering of typewriters and a continuous stream of banter as to who had the best 'exclusive' story and who might land the prized main front-page story – the splash. On a dull news week, stories had to be manufactured so to speak. One of my colleagues who went on to a career in national newspapers demonstrated early promise when he observed on a train journey to work that a number of large trees had been battered in a storm and were hanging perilously over the track. A quick call to the British Railways press office did the trick: 'Train bosses to axe danger trees' was the front page headline the next day.

An abiding memory of the reporters' room is of claustrophobic conditions and tremendous noise, lots of swearing, the clattering of typewriter keys, tobacco smoke and paper. Almost everyone had a cigarette dangling from their lips or balanced precariously on the edge of their typewriter, and perhaps an occasional cigar on pay-day, condemning the news room in the winter when windows could not be opened to a perpetual smoggy haze. By the end of the day ash trays were overflowing, each desk, the bins and much of the floor was covered by screwed-up sheets of discarded copy paper and newspapers and the shelves were stacked with old papers and reference books like Whitaker's Almanack and the Encyclopaedia Britannica, the only means of researching stories way before the internet. Since all the interior office walls were wooden the building was clearly a massive fire trap and we'd occasionally have drills climbing down rickety escape stairs on the outside of the building at the back, an enterprise that I am certain posed almost as many dangers as a fire itself.

Newspaper publishers have built up a reputation over decades for thrift, or perhaps downright meanness might be a better description for an industry guilty at times of poor management and a shocking lack of investment. Several of the typewriters in the reporters' room, including mine, were made in the 1930s, or possibly even earlier. All were manual, the cost of buying electric machines having been dismissed as totally unnecessary. I suppose newspaper owners felt they didn't need to invest as it was ridiculously easy to make money in a large town when papers were really the only viable means of posting advertising for cars, jobs, property, and items for sale.

The paper's library was on the floor immediately above the reporters' room and was overseen by Arthur Cummings, an elderly gentleman who also wrote a popular gardening column and displayed prize-winning flowers at the Reading Show. Arthur doubled as the newspapers' copy-taker, donning headphones to type out stories phoned in by journalists from call boxes across far-flung parts of Berkshire and Oxfordshire.

The library was where you went to find a telephone number by leafing through directories covering every town and city in the country. This was deemed preferable by our bosses to dialling directory inquiries, for which there was a cost.

Today, journalists can 'Google' research instantly by using computer search engines and millions of newspaper cuttings stretching back decades are available digitally. But putting together a cuttings service in the 1970s was a time-consuming labour of love for newspaper librarians who painstakingly snipped out stories of interest each week and placed them in appropriate files. If a reporter wanted to know the history, say, of a long-running planning row, or find out about the career of a leading local councillor or MP, he'd seek out the appropriate file and laboriously go through the cuttings, making a note of matters of interest and taking care to replace everything in the file in the right order when finished.

The library was also the location for a tickertape machine connected to the Press Association in London, which would clatter into action every now and then throughout the day bringing national stories of interest to a regional newspaper. It was this machine that wide-eyed reporters gathered around in 1979 to learn details of the Old Bailey trial of Jeremy Thorpe, the leader of the Liberal Party, who stood accused of conspiring to murder his alleged male lover Norman Scott. Thorpe was acquitted, but the Press Association copy certainly spared no details of the explicit sexual allegations put before the jury, prompting much sniggering among my colleagues at a time when homosexual activity was barely discussed in polite circles, or whispered about if it was mentioned at all.

Reporters typed stories on to sheets of copy paper – two or three paragraphs on each sheet, except for the first paragraph, the 'intro' to the story, which went on one sheet. On the top right-hand corner of the sheet would be written the catchline – a single word to help the subs quickly to identify the story in a basket full of copy. If, for example, you were writing about a council rates rise, an appropriate catchline would obviously be 'rates'. Reporters who attempted to be clever by making up funny catchlines with double-entendres were quickly told by the subs to behave and think again lest their amusing take on matters somehow found itself into the newspaper.

There were to be no more than two paragraphs on each sheet of paper – this enabled a story to be distributed to several typesetters in the composing room, speeding up the process of transferring the story to hot metal. At the bottom of each sheet the reporter had to type MF, for more follows, or MFL for more follows later, to ensure that the sub knew when there would be more to come. When the story was completed, the reporter would type ENDS.

After being checked by the news editor, copy was sent downstairs where subs would edit it, re-write if necessary, and write instructions on the copy paper for the composing room as to the size of typeface and type of font to be used. Some of the more adventurous subs would ask for a WOB, a white on black headline which meant the words of the headline stood out dramatically as they were in white surrounded by a block of black ink. But this involved additional work for the composing room and would be met with resistance by the comp room overseer, back from the pub in combative mood, who would storm into the subs room shouting about it being "too bloody late for any more bloody WOBs" before hurling the copy paper at the chief sub demanding the instruction be rescinded, which it always hastily was as no one dared risk annoying the might of the National Graphical Association (NGA) and a composing room overseer fired up by four or five pints of Morland's best bitter.

Each story had to be copied by placing a piece of carbon paper between two sheets of copy paper. This was known as creating a 'black', a carbon copy that would be kept by the news editor and could later be compared with a subbed version of the story should any questions arise about accuracy or changes to the story made by the subs. The task was all the more difficult if a story was destined for the several district editions of the *Chronicle and Mercury* as well as for the main newspapers. The heavily unionised composing room, run by the NGA, sought to protect jobs by not allowing a single copy of a story to be used for several papers. This meant that three or even four 'blacks' might be needed, which involved hammering the typewriter keys as hard as possible to make sure the fourth 'black' could be read.

The sub-editors were quick to tell us when we had made a mistake and explosions of wrath were not unknown. On one occasion during my early days the reporters' room door burst open, a red-faced sub strode in and without warning, swore loudly, and punched me hard twice on the shoulder. My crime was a grammatical one. I'd repeatedly used a semi-colon when introducing speech quotation marks in a story, rather than a colon: I never made that mistake again.

Chapter Six

Drinking to Excess

The Rising Sun – the Riser – was an ancient Henley Brewery hostelry and the closest pub to the office, which could be reached in less than a minute by exiting the back of the building through the composing room. This made it the pub of choice for thirsty journalists and printers for years. An added advantage was that reporters could sneak out to the Riser without having to go through the main office entrance where the prying eyes of reception staff and the editor's secretary might note who was leaving the building and for how long they were away from their desks.

But the Riser had a brash rival, the White Lion, a modern 1960s building close to Shire Hall and the Crown Courts, a Morland Brewery boozer much favoured by journalists from the freelance Reading News Agency. Ambitious junior reporters like me could try to sell a story to the news agency, or possibly hope to get their name known and earn extra money by landing weekend shifts on Fleet Street papers.

By 1979 I was driving to London and working late-night shifts on the *Daily Mail* while still holding down the *Chronicle* job. Shift workers on the *Mail* arrived at about 6pm for an-eight-hour stint. Our role was to chase around for last-minute stories after the star-name reporters had gone home or departed for the pub. The key moment in any shift occurred around midnight when the first editions of the national newspapers arrived in the office, to be scrutinised by the news desk for any decent stories the *Mail* might have missed. It was then our task to attempt to get a 'new angle' on the missed stories so it appeared to readers that the *Mail* had something fresh and was not merely copying the work of other newspapers.

It was a pretty boring existence for the princely sum of £17 a shift, which even in 1979 was a paltry wage. I quickly decided the Fleet Street bear pit, notorious for ridiculously long hours at work and broken marriages, didn't remotely appeal to someone who wanted to find a wife and have a family.

About this time, I began working weekend shifts at Radio 210, Reading's first independent radio station, writing the news for the Read and Wright show, hosted by DJs Steve Wright and Mike Read. Any thoughts I may have had about moving into broadcasting were dashed. I had the perfect face for radio but, sadly, far from the perfect voice. I also tried my hand at writing news scripts for Southern Television, but the company was based in Southampton and did not see itself as having a long-term future in Reading.

The White Lion, which was frequented by detectives from the town's drug squad, became a popular spot for extended lunch time drinks and for sampling the landlady's extra-hot curries served with a side dish consisting of chopped banana, sultanas and yogurt, which seemed incredibly exotic in the 1970s. When I started, amazingly, the *Chronicle and Mercury*'s composing room overseer, the man in charge of the paper's print process, put in a daily lunchtime shift serving behind the White Lion bar before going back to work. No one appeared to think this the least bit odd, or kept their thoughts to themselves if they did.

If you were a journalist who didn't drink, and preferably in industrial quantities, you were regarded with the utmost suspicion. Half past ten in the morning was a little early for beer, you might think, especially since most of us had only arrived at work 90 minutes earlier, but regular 'early doors' excursions were very much part of the office routine with the favoured hair of the dog to recover from the night before being a 'Worthy' – a bottle of Worthington White Shield, a pale ale with an impressive alcoholic strength of 5.6% ABV. White Shield, which first appeared in 1829 and is still brewed today, is fermented with yeast in the bottom of the bottle so the trick is to pour the contents very carefully into a glass to avoid the yeast tipping in and the beer clouding over. This could be quite a challenge since hungover colleagues whose hands were none too steady ran the risk of ending up with yeast in the glass, something which usually necessitated a quick dash to the nearest toilet shortly after consumption.

Some reporters seeking relief from a mammoth hangover swore by swigging down 20 centilitre bottles of Underberg, a German digestif made from aromatic herbs from forty-three countries with an impressive 44% ABV. This, also, more often than not resulted in departing with the contents of the stomach very quickly.

The drinking culture was very much of its time in the media and in politics. Press briefings, say from companies announcing financial results or expansion plans, were routinely accompanied by limitless free drinks and food, and even councils would arrange for a buffet accompanied by beer and wine when inviting the ladies and gentlemen of the press to attend for important civic announcements.

I remember vividly my only experience of being extremely drunk at work, as opposed to merely merrily pickled. I'd wangled an invitation to a lunchtime reception given by a Reading estate agent celebrating their 100th anniversary. The champagne flowed, I consumed far more than was wise and had to walk back to the office. I collapsed on a bench in a nearby park, unable to move for an hour or so. There were hoots of derision when I finally made it back to the office, but colleagues didn't think the drunken episode was anything out of the ordinary.

This type of thing continued certainly into the early 1990s, after which a new age of moderation and abstinence saw champagne replaced by sparkling bottled water, and press conferences were fuelled by nothing stronger than coffee and tea. Today, my former colleagues tell me, you'd be lucky to get tea and coffee.

By the turn of the century, heavy drinking was a thing of the past on most regional newspapers, although a few older colleagues still felt the need to pop out for some inspirational 'intro juice' when the words just wouldn't flow. There were still rare exceptions to dry lunchtimes, however, and I could only gaze in disbelief when joining the *Birmingham Post* in 2000 at the daily alcohol intake of the Business Desk where boozy 'lunches' often ran from 2pm to about 5.00pm. When they were in the office my new colleagues competed against each other to write the most excruciating puns into the weighty business stories on their computer screens. Automotive firms facing a downturn in profits would have had 'the brakes put on', while a good performance by brewers would inevitably be a case of 'cheers', while railway companies would forever be 'hitting the buffers' and so forth.

In those days the *Post* was a daily morning paper, so business writers returning from their extended visit to the pub were facing another couple of hours of work before they could head home. It was extraordinary they were able to focus on the computer screen, never mind write anything. Somehow, they managed to turn out the required work, and even prided themselves on being able to do so after necking back huge quantities of booze day after day.

Not that any subterfuge was required to have a drink in the 1970s and the 1980s. All that anyone who fancied popping out for a beer had to say was that they were going to meet their 'contacts'. So great was the almost mystical aura of secrecy surrounding 'contacts', the equivalent of a police officer's 'snout' – detectives, councillors, local business leaders, shopkeepers – who you would meet supposedly to glean stories, but essentially to have a drink and a gossip, that no one was ever questioned if they disappeared for an hour or so. This was so ingrained in the newspaper trade that part of my journalism course at Harlow was devoted to compiling a contacts book – a diary, or several diaries, where hacks recorded the telephone numbers of every public figure they might need to get in touch with and took the prized document with them throughout their careers. Acquiring home telephone numbers was regarded as particularly important to enable us to catch people out of the office where they might be more relaxed and amenable to chatting with journalists. Some of my colleagues were incredibly protective of their contacts books and would deny having a home number for, say, the chief of police when you knew full well that they did. Or, they might offer to dial the number out of your sight and then pass the phone over.

And since journalists must never reveal their sources, neither are they required to identify their 'contacts'. Nor, it quickly became obvious to me, did the news editor or chief reporter ever ask whether you'd unearthed any stories from meeting contacts. But if you did happen to come back from a pub with a decent story, you'd be praised to the heavens and told by the very people who had a vested interest in getting out of the office to spend time in a pub that this proved the wisdom of 'meeting real people' and that you'd never uncover any worthwhile stories if you sat behind a desk all day.

There was little in the way of pastoral care on newspapers in the 1970s. Trainees like me had to think on their feet. You were very much on your own and expected to get on with the job. In my experience the best journalists are independent-minded, solitary characters, not given particularly to team working. You might as well try to herd cats as tell journalists what to do. Consequently, there was no question of extended training or help from more experienced colleagues taking new entrants under their wing. Trainees were left pretty much to their own devices in coping with the journalistic jungle. Some survived and prospered. Others fell by the wayside and found something else to do by way of employment.

I was still a trainee when ordered by the news editor to review a classical concert at Reading Town Hall. My protestations that I knew absolutely nothing about classical music were not received sympathetically because journalists were expected to be able to turn their hands to anything. To make matters worse, I'd be writing under the name 'Adagio', a pseudonym for the *Chronicle*'s venerable features editor who for some reason could not review the concert. His dedicated army of highbrow followers would, I felt sure, detect an ill-informed critique so in desperation I hatched a plan. The same concert had been staged a year previously, and was reviewed by Adagio. This meant that the *Chronicle* library would have a cutting of the review, which I simply copied while taking care to make sure my new 'review' mentioned the pieces played when I was at the concert rather than the programme a year previously. Brilliant. No one appeared to notice anything amiss, or if they did there were no complaints to the editor.

Even then, I took something of a risk by leaving the concert half-way through and heading for the pub. It had always been drummed into us at college that we should never leave a play, concert or council meeting early for fear we would miss some earth-shattering event. Stories, mostly apocryphal I am sure, are legendary in newspapers of the hapless reporter turning up at work in the morning and when asked by the editor whether anything interesting had happened at last night's council meeting replying "nothing much", only to be told that he'd missed the mayor dropping down dead or a fire incinerating the town hall.

I was ordered to work one Saturday to write a piece about the Caversham Flower Show, which meant collating the results for the next Friday's paper. This did not suit me at all. Not only was it a mind-numbingly boring assignment, it would have meant cancelling my Saturday morning golf game. I decided to devise what I took to be a fool-proof plan, contacting the show's secretary and arranging for the results to be handed into the *Chronicle* office first thing Monday morning leaving me free to head to the golf club as usual.

The secretary was only too pleased to co-operate and seemed grateful that the show was to receive ample coverage in the local paper. He was as good as his word and the results duly arrived at my desk on Monday. Unfortunately, I failed to notice that they were the wrong results. Unbeknown to me, the secretary, probably flustered by the duty I had imposed on him, managed to hand over the previous year's flower show results, which we duly published. A bit of a row ensued and the *Chronicle* had to apologise and publish the correct results a week later. "Well it's not my fault", was all I could think of saying to colleagues who were highly delighted that my plan collapsed so spectacularly.

Lunch at the *Chronicle and Mercury* would be taken any time between about 12.30 and 2, sometimes extending to 2.30 which was closing time in an era when pub opening times were severely restricted. To celebrate the end of the week several of us would climb into a car on a Friday and head out of town to a country pub for a leisurely session before returning to the office for the afternoon poker school. Some reporters were routinely worse for wear at the end of the week, staggering back to the office literally to sleep it off. One colleague, who went on to hold executive positions in Fleet Street, famously collapsed across three chairs in the reporters' room and was discovered comatose, snoring loudly. He awoke after an hour or so to find his colleagues had covered his clothing with the contents of every ash tray in the room, which was a lot of ash.

It was not unheard of to grab a couple of pints during the morning followed by three or four pints during the lunch break, and then return when the pubs reopened at 5.30 for after-work beers, home for tea and then down to the local pub for more beer. Or, after-work beers followed by an impromptu curry with colleagues and yet more beer.

To a certain extent this relaxed approach to work was possible because the production demands on journalists faced with producing a weekly paper are far less than for those trying to fill daily papers. I recall a rare lunchtime visit to the White Lion by the news editor of the *Reading Evening Post*, who gazed around him in astonishment as pint glasses were being emptied almost as quickly as they could be filled. A *Chronicle* stalwart commented "we work hard, and we play hard", to which the *Evening Post* man replied: "Well, I always see you playing, but I rarely see you working." It was a fair assessment.

In 2000 the Conservative Party leader William Hague attracted guffaws of disbelief when he claimed regularly to have drunk about 14 pints of beer a day as a young man. But he may well have been telling the truth. Certainly, my average daily intake in the late 1970s was at the same striking rate, perhaps even higher.

Then, there were special drink-fuelled outings for the media. I recall attending a press launch at Stratfield Saye, near Basingstoke, magnificent ancestral seat of the Duke of Wellington, where we were entertained by point-to-point horse racing and copious amounts of alcohol. This was the day I discovered Jack Daniel's whisky, resulting in a wiped-out afternoon which finished spectacularly when I ended up sprawled across the front garden at home after bending over in a doomed attempt to stroke the cat. My father, a man with some personal experience of wiped-out afternoons, picked me up and said: "I'd go and lie down if I was you, boy."

An obvious question occurs: was I ever sober? The answer is not after lunch most days. And in a wholly fitting irony, the former *Reading Chronicle* offices in Valpy Street were converted into a wine bar when the paper relocated to new premises out of the town centre.

It pains me to admit it now, but scant attention was paid to drink-driving laws. The Breathalyser, introduced by Barbara Castle in 1967, was still relatively new on the scene and police forces were only beginning to introduce and publicise Christmas and summer crackdowns on drunken drivers. There was a general assumption among some of my colleagues, dangerously incorrect of course, that if you were used to alcohol your body became resistant, you became drink-hardened and could consume three or four pints and still be safe to drive. Reporters often drank with police officers in pubs or at the police club and the officers of the law more than matched us pint for pint, and some drove home.

Most reporters called into the White Lion for a few beers after work. Competition to secure a scoop was fierce and there would often be a mad dash to cover a breaking story – a serious traffic accident, a murder, or public disorder of some sort. A *Chronicle* picture editor became the stuff of legend by asking the police for permission to place a flashing blue light on the roof of his car to speed his way from the pub to assignments. To his utter astonishment, but to no one else's surprise, the request was turned down.

Drinking heavily was by no means confined to the more junior reporters. After one particularly hefty lunchtime session two *Chronicle* editorial executives decided to hold a 'jousting competition' in the narrow corridor running between reception, past the photographic department, and on to the composing room. They faced each other on bicycles armed with golfing umbrellas, but luckily were too worse for wear to inflict any serious injury.

This was very much the culture of the time in newspapers. We were young, most of my colleagues were in their twenties, and we were living the dream in a job perceived by many to be glamorous, for it is true that there is nothing quite as rewarding for the ego than seeing your name sitting proudly above a newspaper story, and anyone who denies that can never have been a decent journalist.

Some of us bought trench coats and copied the way newspaper reporters were portrayed in the movies: hard-drinking, chain smoking and cynical, and we adopted an exaggerated world-weary persona to fit the character. Most of the national newspaper reporters we came across were even harder drinkers, and some paid the ultimate price, drifting into alcoholism and an early death. One national newspaper journalist, probably in his early forties, consumed so much beer during the day that he would often visit the White Lion toilets to be sick in the evening before returning to the bar to drink some more.

Chapter Seven

A Dream Job, and £100 a Week

To say that the pace of life most weekdays was pretty slow in the *Chronicle* office would be an understatement. Reporters would generally take a half-hour afternoon break and head towards a basement café underneath the British Gas showrooms in Friar Street where filter coffees were accompanied by small pots of cream which we used to pour into our cups over the back of a spoon. Coffee and cream. It seemed the giddy height of sophistication at the time.

And while journalism was not remotely in the same pay bracket as, say, accountancy or the law, wages on a newspaper in the late 1970s were reasonable enough for me, a single 23-year-old man still living at home. Senior staff – the chief reporter, news editor, chief sub, sports editor, deputy editor and editor – qualified for company cars with fuel provided for them. Even the crime reporter was given a car when he threatened to take a job on another paper. Sadly, during my entire career in journalism, the perk of a car never winged its way to me. Political reporters, it transpired, were not considered worthy of such benefits.

My pay hit £100 a week in 1980, equivalent to about £560 today after inflation is added on. The average price of a pint of beer in 1976, for example, was 32p, equivalent to £2.50 today, so in real terms beer drinking was a relatively cheap pastime, at least that's my excuse.

There were other advantages, too, including in my case a pass to get into the press box at Elm Park, where Reading FC played, which made me the envy of many soccer-mad friends despite Reading's permanent lowly position in the old third division. And in the late 1970s Reading's newly built Hexagon theatre became the venue for international snooker matches featuring the top names at the time. VIP passes for journalists were easy to come by and enabled us to mix backstage with players such as Ray Reardon, Cliff Thorburn and Alex Higgins and grab a share of the professional snooker lifestyle, essentially as much free booze, food and cigarettes from sponsors Rothmans as you cared to consume.

The Canadian snooker player Bill Werbeniuk claimed to drink forty to fifty pints of lager a day for 'health reasons' – to counteract body tremors, although you might have thought such a prodigious intake of alcohol would make the tremors worse not better. My observations at the time strongly suggest some of Werbeniuk's colleagues were not far behind the Canadian in terms of consumption.

In the late 1970s Porsche Cars opened a dealership in Reading, something that was seen as a significant moment for boosting the town's reputation. Porsche invited local journalists to pair up and test drive some of their fastest and most expensive cars in a day-long rally through Oxfordshire and Berkshire stopping off, unwisely you may think today, at local pubs along the way. Incredibly, even though I'd not long passed my driving test, I was allowed to take part, speeding through the countryside in a car worth many thousands of pounds. We stopped for lunch at the Sir Charles Napier pub in Spriggs Alley, near Chinnor, high up in the Chilterns, where we helped ourselves from the pub's 'draught champagne' tap. Clearly, nothing like that could happen today, and probably that's just as well.

The *Chronicle and Mercury* editorial offices were strategically positioned in Valpy Street at Reading's civic heart, with the magistrates' courts and Town Hall no more than a couple of hundred yards away. The police station, complete with a club and bar to which reporters were sometimes invited for convivial sessions, was next door to the *Chronicle* offices. An easy stroll away were the Shire Hall headquarters of Berkshire County Council and the Crown Court, handily placed next to the White Lion. Reporters could therefore move easily between the office, the pub, and the most important venues for news gathering.

The problem was, the civic heart was about to change. Shortly after I started work, all these rambling expensive to maintain Victorian landmarks closed down and ceased to be public buildings. The Town Hall, police station and magistrates' courts moved to modern purpose-built buildings on the other side of the town centre. The crown court moved out of the town centre which meant reporters now had to drive to get there, or catch a bus. Shire Hall decamped in 1980 to a modern structure at Shinfield Park near the M4 to the south of Reading at a cost of £27.5 million, much to the astonishment of *Reading Chronicle and Berkshire Mercury* readers who wrote angry letters complaining that this was little short of a criminal waste of money at a time when the cost of local government and household rates bills were starting to climb way above inflation.

Such a major reconstruction of the town centre had obvious repercussions in that reporters had to operate further away from the office and it became ever more difficult for news editors to keep tabs on their charges. With mobile phones some twenty-five years into the future, news desks relied on reporters regularly calling in from public phone boxes. Any news desk worth its salt would have a list of the telephone numbers for every conceivable pub in which reporters might be drinking. It wasn't unusual for a landlord to yell out across a crowded bar 'is Paul Dale here? It's the *Reading Chronicle* on the phone', to which a chorus of 'never heard of him' would generally be the response.

Courage's Brewery also moved out of the town centre to a site close to the new Shire Hall, before closing completely in 2010. The relocation put paid to one of Reading's great newspaper traditions – the annual Courage's Christmas party for the media, held at the brewery's own in-house pub on its former town centre site. Clearly, inviting 100 or more journalists to a pub where there is no price list because the beer is free is asking for trouble. And trouble there usually was since the brewery was in the habit of using the occasion to test a new draught ale which invariably was of premium strength. Courage's certainly knew how to organise a piss-up in a brewery.

The format was to arrive at 6pm, hit the free bar for three hours, eat from a generous buffet, then stagger off into the night. Fuelled by alcohol, the going home experience naturally became even more surreal if the streets were frosty or snow-covered. The landlord of the pub opposite the brewery, a Courage inn called The Horn, liked to think of his establishment as something special with its highly polished brasses and comfortable chintzy sofas, and took care to market the place as a watering hole and restaurant for business people and the middle classes. He did not care for journalists, particularly drunken journalists, so the sport for us when the Courage free bar closed was to try to get into The Horn by pretending to be sober. A few made it. Most did not. There were always complaints from the landlord to the editor the following day.

Chapter Eight

Out of the Office and Claiming Expenses

Keeping in contact with reporters who are out of the office has always posed a tough challenge for news editors, given that most journalists are free spirits and instinctively rail against telling their bosses where they are going or who they are going to see. The legendary Dennis 'Nobby' Laxton, who ran the Reading News Agency and joined the *Chronicle* as chief reporter shortly after I started work, possessed a very early battery-powered 'bleeper' which was activated by phone. The number could be dialled from the office and a high-pitched bleeping sound would be emitted from the device in Nobby's pocket much to the astonishment of anyone in earshot. He'd acquired this cutting-edge piece of kit from his friend Ernest Harrison, founder of Berkshire electronics firm Racal, which went on to become Vodafone. This meant that in theory Nobby was always contactable when out of the office, which was most of the time. There was invariably a scribbled note on his desk 'meeting contacts, on bleep' which became legendary and the source of much hilarity since meeting contacts was obviously code for 'out on an extended pub crawl and won't be back until late afternoon'.

Nobby hailed from Yorkshire and was a hard-drinking chain-smoking newspaper man of the old school who referred to his charming wife as 'the head keeper', although probably not in her earshot. His days eking out a living from being a freelance journalist meant he would do whatever it took to secure a story. He claimed to have been so hard-up as a young man when starting work and saving to get married that he couldn't afford to rent a flat, so unbeknown to colleagues crept back into the office at night to secretly sleep on a camp bed which he folded up, hid from his bosses behind a cupboard during the day, and survived on beans on toast cooked in a pan on a two-bar electric fire – at least, that was his story. He swore in later life that chewing raw cloves of garlic was good for his health, much to the distress of anyone standing downwind of him, and his daily consumption of beer would have drunk a small pub dry.

He harboured what would today be regarded as decidedly old-fashioned views about women journalists, although pretty much mainstream for the 1970s. In Nobby's view ladies were good only for light, fluffy feature articles and the appointment by a national newspaper of the first female football writer was written off as a gimmick that wouldn't last. Not that Nobby knew anything about football, or any sport apart, possibly, from horse racing. Once when the Reading News Agency was short staffed, he ended up covering a football match at Elm Park, Reading versus Coventry City, on an exceedingly foggy night. It was by all accounts a poor match and he famously had to ask colleagues the score at the end of the game. He then wrote an excruciating intro along the lines of visibility being so poor that even an appearance on the pitch by a naked Lady Godiva would have gone unnoticed.

Once, following a ghastly murder Nobby turned up at the house of the bereaved family minutes after the star crime reporter from the *Reading Evening Post*, our sworn rivals. The door was slammed in his face and he was denied an interview, but undaunted he followed the *Post* reporter at a safe distance when he left the house and tracked him to a row of public phone boxes. Nobby crept into an adjoining booth where he could hear and write down the *Post* man's interview as he dictated it to his office. Unethical, probably, but resourceful nonetheless.

Finding a telephone to contact the news desk while out of the office on a job could prove difficult. In the case of a police incident, a murder investigation, say, or a serious fire, it was common practice to 'buy' a phone if there was not a public telephone box nearby. This meant knocking on the door of the nearest house and asking for daily use of the person's phone in exchange for, probably, £5. The arrangement wouldn't cost the owner of the phone a penny since all calls to the office were made by transferring the charges. There were even 'exclusivity' arrangements, paying extra to retain use of the phone for the *Chronicle* to exclude reporters from rival publications. Making sure pictures taken from 'staking out' crime scenes or from football matches got back to the office in time for publication was another problem. Reels of film would have to be rushed back to the dark room either by car or by courier motorcycle in a race against time to make the front page 'splash' in the Friday *Chronicle*.

One of the big set-piece occasions for the *Chronicle* was the Reading Show, a chaotic, glorious late-summer celebration of all things agricultural and horticultural, held each year in meadows on the banks of the River Thames where a huge tented village would spring up for all manner of animals, vegetables and flowers to be judged with the winners receiving magnificent silver trophies as well as generous prize money. Inevitably, the show also had quite a few tents devoted purely to selling alcohol which made the event a considerable draw for thirsty farmers from Berkshire and beyond.

The *Chronicle*, which sponsored this prestige event, took the Reading Show very seriously indeed, and coverage had to be planned like a military operation if a full schedule of results was to be published in time for Friday's paper. Each reporter assigned to the show would be given the task of plodding around the tents and writing down the results, but this was a laborious exercise since the number of categories being judged ran into several hundred.

Trainees like me and the more junior reporters were the Reading Show foot-soldiers. Armed with dozens of pieces of copy paper pre-prepared by Arthur in the library with each category typed out – for example, Best Early Potatoes in Show – we'd have to follow in the footsteps of the judges and write down the names of the winner and runners-up. There was much pride involved for the *Chronicle* in getting the results out quickly. Mistakes were unthinkable, but a combination of human error, boredom, and the beer tent, meant that the long list of prize winners was not always as accurate as might have been wished for and the following week's paper generally contained a number of corrections following complaints from prize winners whose names had been incorrectly reported, or worse still, missed out altogether.

Nobby's first and only year in charge of overseeing the Reading Show operation could not be described as an unqualified success. A hard-news man to his fingertips, happiest when reporting on murders and sex scandals, he totally underestimated the logistics of compiling so much mundane information in such a short timescale and, crucially, of making sure a steady stream of completed results was physically transported from the showground back to the *Chronicle* offices about a mile away. There was also the matter of Nobby's vast network of chums who he had arranged to meet and entertain at the show in the beer tents which unlike pubs were allowed to open all day, which was a thing in itself in the 1970s. Looking back, it's not difficult to see that this was a disaster waiting to happen. In the end the results did arrive back at the paper just in time, but Nobby was kept well away from overseeing Operation Reading Show the following year.

The twice-yearly award of 'gongs' to the great and good was another staple diet for local newspapers in the form of the Queen's New Year's Honours at Christmas and the Birthday Honours list in June. But this was a rather trying experience for journalists covering the awards since secrecy surrounding those to be honoured was meant to be watertight. An embargoed list of names would be released to newspapers by the Government 24 hours before publication with all sorts of thinly-veiled threats about the dreadful sanctions that would be imposed on any newspaper breaking the rules by publishing names in advance.

The embargoed list allowed reporters to contact local worthies who were to receive life peerages, knighthoods, OBEs, CBEs, MBEs and suchlike, and allow time for the recipients to tell their story and explain how proud they were to be recognised. But there was a major problem. You were only permitted to talk directly to the person being honoured, and banned from informing anyone else in advance of official publication. This meant it was impossible to tell, say, a PA that you wanted to talk to their boss about an amazing award. Sometimes recipients had briefed their staff in advance that there might be media enquiries, but more often than not those manning the gateway to the captains of industry were blissfully ignorant of what was about to happen and saw no reason to put calls through without a proper explanation from reporters as to why they needed to conduct an interview.

If you did get through the reaction was always pretty much the same. "An incredible surprise. Never dreamt it would happen. Amazing honour. But it's not really for me. It's for my colleagues, my wife, my family etc."

During my first days on the road as a trainee reporter colleagues took the opportunity to impart advice on the art of filling in expenses forms, which translated as 'whatever you do, make sure you keep up and claim as much as everyone else, but don't draw attention to yourself by claiming too much'. Regional newspaper journalists have never been paid vast sums and, as if to make up for this forty years ago, managements largely turned a blind eye to imaginative expenses forms, provided journalists didn't 'take the piss' and attempt to claim an exorbitant amount.

Most newspapers had agreements with the National Union of Journalists that enabled reporters to be paid a set cash sum for lunch or dinner if they were out of the office on a job, without having to provide a receipt to prove that a meal had actually been purchased. This meant there was quite an incentive to make sure you were away from your desk and on a job of some sort where you could buy some cheap sandwiches but still claim for a lunch thereby swelling the wage packet. During my first couple of weeks after being freed from the captivity of the subs' room I accompanied a senior reporter to a press briefing at Thames Valley Police headquarters at Kidlington near Oxford. We stopped off at a pub for lunch on the way back, which in my naivety I was astonished to learn would be paid for by the *Chronicle*. Scampi and chips were consumed and I still remember the look of astonishment on my parents' faces when I told them I had a job that provided free food and beer in pubs.

Claims could be made for 'entertaining' contacts, generally councillors and council officers in my case, and receipts were not required until way into the mid 1990s. One way of looking at it is that a journalist's word that he had spent, say, £5 on drinks and food was good enough in those more innocent and trustworthy days. In reality though I'm sure newspaper managements knew they were being taken for a ride but were prepared to lose a relatively small amount of money on 'imaginative' expenses claims as long as salaries could be kept depressed, which they certainly were. This interesting state of affairs lasted until the end of the 20th century when newspaper groups, now more often than not part of publicly quoted companies, came more and more under the control of accountants who did not look kindly upon expenses for journalists, or wage increases for that matter.

We could only gaze in envy at the lucrative arrangements that existed for the national newspaper journalists working on our patch who were, for example, able to claim a hefty weekly allowance for buying daily newspapers with no receipts required, of course, plus seemingly unlimited amounts for 'entertaining contacts'. Stories of Fleet Street expenses fiddles were legendary. It was common practice for hacks from different newspapers who were out on the same job to pool their claims by going to a restaurant and asking for a single bill for, say, four people rather than splitting the cost individually. They'd then persuade the waiter to provide four identical receipts, each one listing the total cost of the meal. For example, if the total cost of the meal was £60 the proper procedure would have been to ask for four £15 receipts. What actually happened was that each reporter walked away with a receipt for £60 which he would claim for when returning to his office, thereby cashing in on a tidy £45 profit.

Expenses arrived at the *Chronicle* editorial floor on Friday mornings, just in time for lunchtime frivolities, in the form of cash stuffed into little white envelopes. The reporters most adept at claiming were quick to pull out and show off £5 notes with gleeful shouts of 'it's a bluey' before heading for the pub to spend the fruits of their labours. It's not difficult in such circumstances to see that some of my colleagues ended up relying on their expenses to boost the weekly wage, perhaps by as much as a third, and were to suffer swingeing cuts in pay and real hardship when the expenses bandwagon ceased to roll on regional newspapers in the 1990s.

When I first joined the *Chronicle*, wages were paid weekly and in cash. After a while, a weekly cheque was introduced and could be taken to be cashed at a nearby bank. There was no system for paying salaries directly into bank accounts until the late 1980s.

One of my earliest assignments on the *Chronicle and Mercury* offered an interesting insight into the character of a leading sportsman. In the late 1970s Geoffrey Boycott, the England opening batsman, was involved in one of his periodic spats with Yorkshire County Cricket Club. We were tipped off that the great man had agreed to turn out for an obscure village side deep in the Oxfordshire countryside, and as I played cricket for a village team in south Oxfordshire, I was chosen as a suitable person to attend the match and attempt to get an interview with Boycott.

In the days before GPS and Satellite Navigation a journey into the woods and winding lanes of Oxfordshire inevitably involved much stopping and consulting of maps, but eventually I arrived at a picture-perfect English country cricket ground, to find a BBC reporter and film crew waiting. This was not going to be an exclusive story for the *Chronicle*.

Boycott emerged from the pavilion and made his way towards the film crew. The first thing I noticed was that he was wearing luminous blue contact lenses which were unsettling to say the least. I approached and asked him for a chat.

He replied: "How much are you going to pay then?"

I explained that newspapers like the *Reading Chronicle* didn't pay for interviews, which was true. That didn't go down very well, but Boycott kindly agreed to my suggestion that I could sit in on the BBC reporter's interview and take notes. I was pretty sure that the BBC would use only a brief clip from Boycott on the television news, but that the reporter would ask lots of questions. That turned out to be the case so I had extensive quotes from the cricketer, which pleased the *Chronicle* news desk. I took the view that discretion was the better part of valour, so didn't mention that, strictly speaking, the interview was the BBC's and not mine.

Chapter Nine

Our Man at the Town Hall

A t the end of the 1970s and into the 1980s, both the *Reading Chronicle* and *Berkshire Mercury* were still attempting to provide a weekly news service taking in most of Berkshire and Oxfordshire and had several reporters covering a district patch who generally worked from home, although there was a district office in Henley-on-Thames. One of my first regular jobs after passing the driving test and buying a car was to cover Bracknell magistrates' court on a Monday and Tuesday and to attend meetings of Wokingham District Council in the evenings, which was a promotion from the tedious parish councils whose meetings I had previously been assigned to. Nobby took me to one side and told me I'd been singled out for the Bracknell and Wokingham patch because "your mobility has been recognised". I replied: "Did you say my ability has been recognised?" Nobby, deadpan: "No, son ... I said your mobility."

This was a handy posting for two reasons. The forty-four mile round trip between Reading and Bracknell plus regular evening visits to Wokingham for council meetings did wonders for my weekly mileage expenses claims and, even better, I was out of the office for two days and left entirely to my own devices. My bosses would be pleased as long as I returned with a few juicy court cases, and you could hardly fail to do so in the rough New Town of Bracknell. And as a bonus, if the court wrapped up by noon as it generally did, there was no need whatsoever to tell the news desk that proceedings had finished early. A leisurely journey home could take in a country pub or two before arriving at the office by about 3pm, leaving a couple of hours to write-up the court copy before heading to the White Lion for early doors at 5.30. Rule number one for reporters: never get back to the office until absolutely necessary. Rule number two: never tell anyone where you are unless absolutely necessary.

Following the retirement of Bill Garner, deputy editor Chris Girdler was appointed editor. But Girdler's period in charge swiftly came to an abrupt end when Argus Press bought the *Reading Chronicle* and *Berkshire Mercury* from the newspapers' private shareholders. The disposal, which had been kept a closely guarded secret, came as a huge shock to pretty much everyone at the

Chronicle and *Mercury* and prompted Girdler to head up a campaign to halt the sale and keep the newspapers in family hands.

Bravely, he used his own newspaper to explain on the front page why he didn't think selling to a national conglomerate like Argus Press was a good idea. Girdler toured the country attempting to find a more suitable buyer, even approaching the tycoon Roland 'Tiny' Rowland, but it was no good and the sale to Argus Press went through. Unsurprisingly, Girdler left the company shortly afterwards and became one of the founders of Paragon Press, a London-based PR and publishing company. His place as editor was taken by an Argus Press executive, Kimble Earl, a tall, loud man, with huge sideburns and a penchant for wearing Union Jack socks.

Girdler, meanwhile, kindly gave me some shifts at Paragon Press's offices near Oxford Circus, for which I earned far more than my weekly wage at the *Reading Chronicle*. But the world of PR and writing puff pieces about Birds Eye peas and Mars Bars was not for me even if the money was good.

It is generally recognised that what goes on in the country's town halls has always been and always will be the life blood of local newspapers, whether printed or online versions. What councils do, or fail to do, impacts on our lives in so many ways, from emptying dustbins and street cleaning to mending the roads, maintaining parks, running libraries and schools, granting planning permission – so many opportunities for controversy and a juicy news story.

It is also true that, like most people, very few journalists are remotely interested in local government. In fact, many of my colleagues over the years would have willingly sold their grandmother to avoid having to attend a council meeting. But every cloud has a silver lining and for someone like me who had been fascinated by politics from a fairly young age the opportunity to get immersed in the activities of town halls, and to be paid for doing so, was too good to resist.

I'd hardly been at the *Chronicle* for two years when an opportunity arose to become the local government reporter, with a remit to write about the affairs of Reading Borough Council and Berkshire County Council. It's fair to say there was hardly a queue of contenders beating a path to the editor's door. In fact, I think I was the only person to show any interest. Unsurprisingly, I got the job. And a small pay rise.

One obvious advantage of my new post immediately became clear and paid dividends over the years. I would be left pretty much alone by news editors who, while realising that stories from councils were bread and butter for their newspapers, generally had little understanding of how councils actually operated or even much of an interest in local politics. Provided the local government man could come up with a steady stream of decent stories (and it was invariably a man back then) he could spend as much time out of the office as he liked, which suited me down to the ground.

Political control of Reading Borough Council switched regularly between Labour and the Conservatives from 1973 to 1983 with neither party managing to secure an overall majority in the chamber and generally relying on support from a handful of Liberals to form an administration. Berkshire County Council was resolutely Tory, stuffed with retired wing commanders and rear-admirals, although Labour and the Liberals were beginning to make inroads.

I immediately felt at home and knew instinctively that the rest of my career in journalism would be spent writing about the affairs of councils. The long hours weren't a concern and I even spent most Saturday lunchtimes drinking with some of Reading's more media-friendly Labour councillors in an effort to get the inside track on emerging stories.

Council and committee meetings were held in the evenings in Reading and went on for a long time thanks to political point scoring between the three sides, although the politicians made sure they were usually finished just before the pubs shut at 10.30, for obvious reasons. The council had recently moved to new open plan offices to the west of the town centre and in true local government fashion at that time no expense had been spared in kitting out the building, including an impressive press gallery with expensive leather armchairs where we could sit comfortably and observe the antics of councillors in the chamber below.

It was in the press gallery that I committed a stupid act that could have brought my career in political journalism to an abrupt end. Sitting next to a colleague from the *Reading Evening Post*, who went on to become a senior newspaper manager in Fleet Street, we both agreed that the council's committee proceedings were even more tedious than usual. For some unfathomable reason I made a paper aeroplane and wrote a message on the wings: "You are all so boring, why don't you just sod-off and go home." I grasped the piece of paper attempting to flick it to my friend, but to the horror of both of us the plane took a nosedive and came to rest at the very edge of the press gallery balcony, perilously close to fluttering down into the midst of transportation committee members, who were not known for possessing a sense of humour particularly where journalists were concerned and were in any case after my blood for a series of articles exposing the ballooning cost of building Reading's ring road, the Inner Distribution Road.

The middle of the 1970s saw local government facing another of its regular financial crises as demand for services, particularly social care, began to grow. In 1975, the Labour Environment Secretary Tony Crossland, speaking at Manchester Town Hall, issued a blunt message to town halls, interpreted by the media along the lines of "the party is over". His clear warning to council was that they would have to trim spending in the light of a growing economic crisis.

This is what Crossland said: "For the next few years times will not be normal. Perhaps people have used the words economic crisis too often in the past. They have shouted wolf when the animal was more akin to a rather disagreeable Yorkshire terrier. But not now. The crisis that faces us is infinitely more serious than any of the crises we have faced over the past twenty years ... With its usual spirit of patriotism and its tradition of service to the community's needs, it is coming to realise that, for the time being at least, the party is over ... We are not calling for a headlong retreat. But we are calling for a standstill."

His message shocked Labour-run councils to the core, although it should be pointed out Crossland wasn't suggesting the amount of Government money handed to local authorities should be reduced, simply that the year-on-year increase, often above inflation, had to be stopped.

This was the start of a trend for local government that would play out over the next forty years and still shows no sign of easing. One of my first assignments as local government reporter was to attend a meeting of the newly formed Reading Ratepayers' Association, an organisation claiming to be non-political that had been formed to challenge soaring household rates bills and demand better value for money from councils, although it is fair to say that most members made little secret of their Conservative sympathies. Ratepayers groups were springing up across the country and beginning to put their own candidates forward for election to councils in a direct challenge to the main political parties, although only a very few ratepayers' representatives ever managed to break the mould and get themselves elected.

The meeting drew local media attention because it was addressed by Reading council chief executive William Henry 'Harry' Tee, a blunt Northerner who in 1967 had become the youngest local authority chief of any borough council in the country. Known locally by the nickname Mr Reading, Tee ruled the politicians with an iron grip and had a straightforward message for the ratepayers: the government expects councils to provide more and more in the way of public services, so your rates bill will continue to rise above inflation. Tee's speech was highly controversial at the time because it came from an unelected council official who was not supposed to deliver 'political' messages.

The *Chronicle* news editor was so concerned about this, questioning whether I had correctly interpreted Tee's remarks, that he insisted I phone the chief executive to check my story with him, which I did. Tee, who drove a Jaguar with a personalised number plate DP1, DP being the registration mark for Reading, could not be described as publicity-shy. He turned out to be more than happy with the *Chronicle*'s take on his speech.

Reading hit the national headlines in 1978, but for all the wrong reasons when an eight-year-old boy, Lester Chapman, ran away from home and disappeared. Following an avalanche of national publicity and days of searching, in which hundreds of volunteers joined police to scour fields and remote spots, little Lester's body was found in a pit of sludge where he had frozen to death. A subsequent inquiry uncovered a pattern that was to become all too familiar across the country over the next four decades – Lester had been known to the police and both Berkshire and Hampshire social services but a lack of co-operation between public agencies and a failure to share information enabled him to slip through the net with horrific consequences.

The case was remarkable in that it attracted massive attention on television news and in the national press long before interest in such incidents could be stirred up via social media and provoked a storm of comment from MPs and local councillors along the lines of 'something like this must never be allowed to happen again'. Sadly, there have been a great many other children like Lester Chapman since then whose lives have been lost largely as a result of social services, schools and police failing to share information with each other.

Inevitably, Berkshire county council ordered a formal inquiry into the tragedy. A report, running into more than 100 pages detailing the failings of the authorities was to be published and I was determined the *Chronicle and Mercury* should secure a scoop by obtaining a copy of the document before anyone else. Having discovered that publication was imminent I walked into the printing room at Shire Hall and casually asked for a copy of the Lester Chapman report. As I surely ought to have predicted, my identity was questioned and I beat a hasty retreat back to the office by which time the council's press officer was already screaming down the phone to the news desk about the unethical behaviour of Paul Dale. Nothing much happened as a result, although my bosses did make it clear such behaviour by a reporter was probably unwise.

Chapter Ten

1979 General Election

In 1979 I covered my first General Election and witnessed Margaret Thatcher deliver a resounding Tory victory against a Labour party whose public support had ebbed away during months of militant trade unionism and disruption to public services which became known as the Winter of Discontent.

Labour had high hopes of gaining Reading North and Reading South but both constituencies were fairly easily retained by the Conservatives with Tony Durant holding his seat in the north of the town and Dr Gerard Vaughan being returned in the south. Durant recognised the importance of keeping the local media onside and had excellent relations with the *Chronicle and Mercury*, always making himself available for a chat either on the phone or in person, and was also a dedicated proponent of self-promotion through newspaper photo-opportunities generally involving the MP looking grim-faced at pot holes in the road or shaking a fist at broken pedestrian crossings.

Durant's seat was thought to be the more vulnerable of the two Reading constituencies to challenge by Labour and several senior Conservative figures were shipped in to support his campaign, including Sir Keith Joseph, who at that time was Mrs Thatcher's head of policy and research and a key adviser. The cerebral Sir Keith, who became a Fellow of All Souls, Oxford, at the age of 28, and was once spoken of as a future Tory leader, had blotted his copybook when giving a controversial speech in Birmingham in 1974 in which he appeared to dabble in the area of eugenics by suggesting poor parents should somehow be prevented from having families because their children were likely to be of low intelligence.

This was what Joseph said:

"A high and rising proportion of children are being born to mothers least fitted to bring children into the world ... Some are of low intelligence, most of low educational attainment. They are unlikely to be able to give children the stable emotional background, the consistent combination of love and firmness ... They are producing problem children ... The balance of our human stock, is threatened."

The best that can be said of the speech is that it was clumsy. In reality, the Orwellian tone of his remarks, especially the sinister "the balance of our human stock is threatened", was a cataclysmic error by Joseph whose career never recovered and was portrayed thereafter in the media as crazy, not far removed from supporting Nazi ideology, and earned the nickname The Mad Monk in a reference to the Russian mystic Rasputin whose malign influence over the Tsar was feared and resented by the royal court.

Sir Keith gave a press conference at Tony Durant's house in Caversham. The occasion was remarkable for a cameo appearance by a reporter from *The Times*, even though the newspaper was mid-way through a year-long shutdown during a bitter industrial dispute with the print unions and was therefore not published during the general election campaign. We were about five minutes into the media briefing when there was a knock on the door: "The gentleman from the *Times* is here, Sir."

Joseph was immediately on his feet. "Ah, good, show him in. Show him in."

The *Times* reporter was warmly greeted by Joseph and Durant and treated reverentially even though the notes he took would never see the light of day in the newspaper. The odd incident was an early indication to me of the importance attached by the political establishment to newspapers like *The Times* whose representatives clearly still managed to attract the attention of the country's leaders even though it hadn't published a single edition for months.

The election count at Reading Town Hall, my first, was memorable only because the borough council managed to lose a ballot box from Reading North. As the night dragged on into the early hours, television crews began to drift away when results from across the country made it clear that Mrs Thatcher was heading for victory and there were unlikely to be any Labour gains in Reading, and precious few anywhere else for that matter. In the end, as the missing ballot papers could not be located, we all went home and had to return the following day for the Reading North count to resume after the box had been found and for Durant's victory to be confirmed.

The election campaign gave me my first chance to write about national politics, and there could hardly have been a better way to start than interviewing Denis Healey, a towering giant of the post-war Labour movement who was Chancellor of the Exchequer in the dying days of Jim Callaghan's government.

Healey had been sent out on a tour of marginal seats in the Thames Valley, with Reading North identified as a key target for Labour. With the benefit of hindsight, most political commentators have convinced themselves that a Conservative victory in the 1979 General Election was always likely, given the political damage heaped on the Labour government by the Winter of Discontent. But it didn't seem that way at the time, and there were plenty of people who thought it highly unlikely Britain would ever elect a woman as prime minister and that voters would opt instead for 'better the devil you know' and return the avuncular Jim Callaghan to Downing Street.

As the recently appointed local government reporter, I was the closest the *Reading Chronicle and Berkshire Mercury* had to a political reporter and was duly dispatched by the news editor to the railway station at very short notice to "get a few words with Mr Healey".

The unmistakable bulky figure of Denis Healey on his own, as the Chancellor did not qualify for special branch protection while not on government duty in those dim and distant days, emerged from the train to be greeted by a nervous reporter, with no sign of anyone from the Labour party on the platform. Introductions over, Healey explained "don't worry this sort of thing happens all the time, they're probably outside".

Outside they were, with an ancient Rover car to take Healey to the local street market where he conducted a rumbustious walkabout, and then on to the local party headquarters for lunch and media interviews. The car wouldn't start when he came to leave, and we pushed it down the road to get the engine going, with a beaming Chancellor sitting inside clearly enjoying the spectacle.

I last saw Denis Healey when covering the 1983 General Election campaign for the *Oxford Mail*. He had been persuaded, although very little persuasion was needed, to play some lively tunes on a piano at an Oxfordshire old folks' home. Although he was a very senior Labour figure who would probably have become Chancellor or Foreign Secretary had Neil Kinnock managed to win the 1983 election, Healey entered willingly into the part of amiable fool – which could not have been further from the truth – joking with admirers and even allowing a lucky few to touch the famous eyebrows.

The description 'larger than life' could have been invented for Denis Healey. The Labour movement ran through his blood, but he had a substantial life outside of politics and was a well-rounded man with a love for life and a huge cultural hinterland. He was, in fact, the polar-opposite of some of today's professional politicians who know little of life beyond Westminster.

He could talk to people, young or old, bright or not so bright, without any requirement for spin or prepared scripts, never turned down the opportunity for a full and frank discussion, and was even gifted a "you silly billy" catchphrase by the impressionist Mike Yarwood, which rather than being upset about he used to his advantage.

My last six months at the *Chronicle and Mercury* were spent back in the subs' room where I was introduced to the art of subbing and page-layout. For reasons that have never been clear to me journalists wishing to be promoted to management roles are usually required to do so through a subbing route rather than as writers. I rather fancied becoming an editor at the time, but found desk-bound subbing not to my liking and rather boring.

There was however one compensation to returning to the subs room. The *Chronicle* had recently opened a free weekly paper which although distributed in Reading was typeset and printed in Edenbridge, Kent. This meant a day out for me and another sub, driving down to Kent to "see the paper off the stone" with the added attraction sometimes of staying overnight in a hotel at the company's expense. To amuse ourselves we set out to see how quickly we could travel from Reading to Edenbridge in a rather battered company mini, often reaching 80mph on the Kingston bypass in the days before speed cameras. The record for the fifty-nine mile trip was about fifty minutes, from memory.

A year after the 1979 General Election I became aware that the *Oxford Mail* and *Oxford Times* were in the market for a new local government reporter. I applied, got the job with a substantial pay rise, and left for the last time my home town of Reading in the summer of 1980.

Part III

Oxford 1980-1986

Chapter Eleven

Dreaming Spires

The Victorian poet Matthew Arnold waxed lyrical about Oxford, writing from the high ground of Boars Hill, gazing at the university churches and colleges in the distance: "And that sweet City with her dreaming spires. She needs not June for beauty's heightening."

What is often not quoted is the rather more critical way Arnold continued his assessment of Oxford: "Home of lost causes, and forsaken beliefs, and unpopular names, and impossible loyalties!"

William Wordsworth, although a Cambridge man, was also captivated by Oxford's bewitching beauty:

"Yet, O ye spires of Oxford! Domes and towers!
"Gardens and groves! Your presence overpowers
"The soberness of reason;"

You'd need to be a particularly dull philistine not to be captivated by the beguiling nature of Oxford with its stunning architecture and the timeless beauty of the university colleges. I spent six years there, first as local government correspondent and then public affairs correspondent for the *Oxford Mail and Oxford Times*. I really didn't want to leave but it dawned on me that a comfortable existence in the city's political and academic life contained few challenges for a journalist who wanted to make a mark (and try to make some money), but as the poets found, it did have a great many pleasant distractions with a real risk of overpowering the soberness of reason.

Walk along High Street, said by some to be the most beautiful city high street in Britain, and take in scenes that have changed little in 200 years – undergraduates in gowns cycling furiously on their way to lectures, bowler-hatted 'Bulldogs', the university's own police force, standing guard at the college entrances allowing the public only the merest glimpse of the finely cut lawns bordering magnificent buildings dating back to the 14th century.

Shop in the indoor market where it is possible to buy anything from a live lobster to a jar of caviar. Stroll across The Parks and watch free of charge the

University playing cricket against the visiting tourists. Meander along the banks of the Isis during May to take in the spectacle of student rowing teams competing in Eights Week and enjoy a Pimms or two in one of the many refreshment tents; the whole place resembles a film set, the type of exaggerated picture of Oxford that Disney Studios might present. Except that this is real life, or as close to real life as it is possible to get in Oxford.

The Tory prime minister Lord Salisbury summed up Oxford's distractions accurately in 1900: "If I had to do literary work of an absorbing character, Oxford is the last place in which I should attempt to do it."

Kenneth Grahame, writing *The Wind in the Willows* eight years later, took a sideswipe at Oxford's pretensions: "The clever men at Oxford know all that there is to be knowed. But they none of them know one half as much as intelligent Mr Toad!"

When I arrived at the *Oxford Mail and Oxford Times* in 1980 many editorial staff had joined pretty much straight from university, from Oxford University naturally. There were though others, older members of staff, mainly ex-grammar school boys who had come up through the ranks of regional journalism and were nearing retirement age. One of these, who eventually became chief sub on the *Oxford Mail*, had a legendary reputation for failing to spot double-entendres in the copy he was checking and re-writing. He became the unwitting subject of much hilarity in the newsroom having penned a questionable headline to capture prime minister Harold Wilson's attempts to take on leaders of the National Union of Seamen, whose members were engaged in a damaging national strike: "Wilson puts seamen on the carpet." The double meaning had to be carefully explained to the sub, who must have lived a sheltered life.

Anthony 'Tony' Price, editor of the weekly *Oxford Times*, was a Merton College man and on most days proudly wore his college tie to work. Quite a few of the senior editorial staff had been at Oxford University with Price, a friendly clubbable fellow with an impressive network of contacts in high places, who set his career on track in the 1950s by securing the first newspaper interview with *Lord of the Rings* author JRR Tolkein, an Oxford Don.

Price, who died aged 90 in 2019, wrote well-received thrillers in his spare time winning the Crime Writers' Association of Great Britain Silver Dagger and Gold Dagger awards for his Dr David Audley/Colonel Jack Butler series of books based loosely on MI5 and counter-espionage. Note the words 'spare time', for I cannot believe editing the newspaper he was in charge of could have been a particularly arduous job. Indeed, to prove the point, he managed to turn out 20 books in as many years during his career at the *Oxford Times*.

The *Oxford Times* was founded in 1862 and liked to think of itself as Oxfordshire's premier publication read by the university and county set, certainly a bit above the more blue-collar *Oxford Mail*. Under Price's editorship it was very much the voice of north Oxford ladies and Dons, especially where environmental matters were concerned, and could always be called upon to campaign strongly against any attempts by the city council to approve 'unsuitable' housing or industrial development. There were long and largely successful campaigns against intrusion into the green belt and a notable defeat of controversial county council proposals to build a southern Oxford bypass across the historic Christ Church Meadows in the 1970s.

A unique claim to fame was that in 1922 T E Lawrence, better known as Lawrence of Arabia, commissioned the *Oxford Times* to typeset and print an advanced private edition of *The Seven Pillars of Wisdom*, an autobiographical account of his military service in Arabia. Lawrence's younger brother, although very old by 1980, lived in Oxford and kept in touch with Tony Price, thus underlining the newspaper's sense of history and tradition.

The *Oxford Times* was very picky about the reporting of university affairs. Woe betide any reporter who referred to 'Queen's College' rather than 'The Queen's College'. You'd also be expected to know that Christ Church (two words) is the only university college in the world which is also a cathedral, is known in Oxford as 'The House', and must never be referred to as Christ Church College, or even worse as Christchurch. St Edmund Hall, in an eternal battle with University College, Merton and Balliol as to which is the oldest college in Oxford, is known to its undergraduates and graduates as 'Teddy Hall', and Magdalen College is pronounced 'Maudlin', but most people know that.

The *Oxford Mail* was an evening newspaper and its editor could hardly have been more of a contrast to the Oxbridge set. Terry Page hailed from London and had earned a reputation as a brilliant young sub on Fleet Street papers before editing the *Brighton Argus* from where he was head-hunted to give the *Oxford Mail* a fresh start.

In common with the *Reading Chronicle* and *Berkshire Mercury*, and most other regional newspapers, alarm bells were ringing over rapidly diminishing sales. Page was appointed to oversee the *Oxford Mail*'s transformation from broadsheet to tabloid, taking over from Mark Barrington-Ward, son of the war-time editor of *The Times* and brother of the Bishop of Coventry. Educated at Eton College and Balliol College, Barrington-Ward, or 'Crashington-Bore' as one reporter cruelly nicknamed him, was regarded as something of an intellectually aloof figure in the news room and was certainly not suited to the banter and rough and tumble of regional newspapers. He eventually found himself promoted sideways to become *Westminster Press*'s political editor at Westminster in order to create an opening for Page.

Page was charged with stopping the circulation from continuing to ebb away and, most unusually for a regional newspaper at that time, the move from broadsheet to tabloid was backed by an expensive television advertising campaign. The aim was partly to move the paper on from its sales base in Oxford's car factories, which were mostly closing down anyway, and also to give it a wider family appeal, particularly among women. Most people in the office feared Page was there simply to take the paper down-market.

Page left Oxford while I was still there to become editor of the *Sunday Mercury* in Birmingham where he was a key figure in the management buyout of *The Birmingham Post*, *Birmingham Evening Mail*, *Coventry Evening Telegraph* and the *Sunday Mercury* from the American publisher Ralph Ingersoll. The subsequent stock market flotation of Midland Independent Newspapers turned Terry into a wealthy man and he retired to Spain.

Chapter Twelve

Mail and Times – Keen Rivals

Tony and Terry had offices on the open plan *Mail and Times* editorial floor where they could sit behind glass partitions and stare at each other and where everyone else on the editorial floor could see inside, unless the blinds were drawn, which inevitably stirred up speculation about what was going on. In fact, despite an age gap of about 20 years between the younger Page and the older Price, they got on well even though there was a fierce competitive rivalry between the two papers.

My arrival prompted something of a buzz in the news room. For a start, I was only 24 which was precociously young to be a local government reporter in *Oxford Mail and Times* terms. And not only was I not an Oxbridge graduate, I hadn't even been to university. I was fully aware several of my new supposedly better educated work colleagues had applied for the local government role and would be eyeing me suspiciously and quite possibly resentfully, and that proved to be the case at first. I addressed this in the only way I knew, getting my head down, working hard, and leading by example.

I was expected to provide exclusive council stories for the weekly *Oxford Times* as well as a steady flow of council stories for the *Oxford Mail* on a daily basis. This was a task that called for a certain amount of diplomacy and an ability to keep stories destined for the *Oxford Times* well away from the grasping hands of the *Mail*'s editorial executives. Matters were not helped by the fact that both papers shared a composing room which had moved on dramatically from the days of hot metal, with stories now being cut and pasted on to pages ready for printing. For the *Mail*, a daily paper, this was of course a non-stop process for six days a week. But the weekly *Times*, published on Friday but printed on a Thursday night, would start to paste-up its news pages on the previous Monday. This meant that *Mail* editorial executives could stroll through the composing room and keep an eye out to see whether the *Oxford Times* had any decent stories for the coming Friday that the *Mail* had missed, and then complain to the news desk if this was the case.

It was claimed that the *Oxford Times* once had a big story which it wanted to keep from the *Mail*, so Tony Price arranged for two versions to be prepared – one, the actual story, was kept back until the last minute, and a spoof alternative story written entirely in Latin was pasted on to a page in the composing room. This is probably an apocryphal tale, although I wouldn't be entirely surprised if it turned out to be true. It's the sort of eccentric thing that happened at Oxford.

I began my leader-writing career at the *Oxford Times*, penning the editorial comment column setting out the paper's view on the big local and sometimes national issues of the day, a task I relished as it gave me a certain amount of power to set the paper's editorial policy. This was something I would continue to do at the *Coventry Evening Telegraph* and, most notably, at the *Birmingham Post* where I wrote the majority of leading articles between 2000 and 2010, including the paper's initial reaction to the 9/11 terrorist atrocities in America.

Tony Price was happy to give me a brief outline of the stance he wanted to take on issues of the week, generally involving the shortcomings of the city or county council, and leave it to me to provide 500 words. The *Oxford Mail* leaders, far shorter and snappier than the *Oxford Times*'s, were written and jealously guarded by deputy editor Colin Dobson, whose public image in the office was that of a dour, prickly Yorkshire man, but who was in fact a well-read and amenable colleague, especially after a few pints. He would often ask me to read through editorials he had written about the city council, stressing sternly: "Check me for facts. Just check for facts, mind." The message was clear enough: facts were my domain; opinion was his.

I began to write a weekly political column for the *Oxford Times*, something I would continue to do for 30 years while I was at Oxford and then the *Coventry Evening Telegraph* and *The Birmingham Post*. My approach was always the same – a mix of serious political comment and gossip, in an attempt to amuse and inform readers and to prick the pomposity and often sizeable egos of our elected representatives. Writing a column was something I'd wanted to do for some time, but the *Oxford Mail* already had a punchy weekly column so I sensed the paper wouldn't be particularly interested in a second. I concentrated instead on the *Oxford Times*, where Tony Price didn't require much persuading. I handed him a mock-up of my first potential column, about three or four short stories, and very shortly 'Dale's Diary' was a regular feature of the *Times*'s offer to readers. I quickly discovered that a great many politicians, whatever they might say in public about scandalous media gossip, privately relished appearing in the column, and some were quite miffed if several weeks went by and they didn't get a mention. There was never any shortage throughout my career of council members, officials and MPs passing on tips for the column, often at the expense of their colleagues.

There were regular Friday lunchtime drinks with the two editors and senior staff to which I was routinely invited. This relationship did not help to change the minds of certain of my more left-wing news room colleagues who regarded me as a right-wing and rough-edged upstart. They'd now convinced themselves that I was a management stooge as well.

We'd drive in a convoy of cars to the Eight Bells at Eaton, a picturesque country pub between Oxford and Abingdon, for a convivial session to wind down at the end of the week and were often joined by key figures from politics, businesses, and the University. Douglas Hurd, the Old Etonian former Tory Foreign Secretary and Home Secretary, who was MP for the Oxfordshire constituency of Witney, came once with his visit remembered largely because he brought no money with him or means to pay for a round of drinks, or if he did his wallet stayed firmly in his pocket.

It was during a visit to the Eight Bells that it was suggested I might like to do a little unofficial undercover work for the Government – although the approach wasn't put anywhere near as bluntly as that. A well-known and highly respected figure with direct links to the University took me to one side to talk about the latest spate of "dreadful" strikes at the city's Cowley car plants. The point he wanted to stress was the damage that "Trotskyist" shop stewards could inflict on the economy and the country if trade union extremism in Oxford spread across British industry.

The Tory Government, my drinking companion continued, was naturally very concerned about this and was worried in particular by several stories in the *Oxford Mail* claiming that a far-left subversive, dubbed 'The Mole' by the paper, was working on the car assembly track at Cowley with a view to stirring up dissent and industrial unrest among the workforce. Might I be in a position, given my political and trade union contacts, to gather relevant information and pass it on to people who could make use of it? "You wouldn't be out of pocket for your time and trouble, of course," he added smoothly.

The offer was made in such a quiet matter of fact way on a hot summer's day in a quintessentially English country pub with roses growing around the door that it didn't occur to me until later that I'd almost certainly been tapped up on behalf of the security services. This may sound utterly far-fetched, like something out of a cold war thriller, but it is important to recall that Britain in 1982 was a country in political turmoil where the post-war tax and spend consensus between Conservative and Labour was giving way to sharply polarised politics of right and left courtesy of Margaret Thatcher and Michael Foot.

Only a few years before, in the mid-1970s, rumours had circulated in the media about plans for an army-backed coup planned against the Labour government of Harold Wilson. Tensions were heightened by rogue MI5 agents and the head of the CIA at the time, James Angleton, who believed that Wilson was a Soviet spy, although no justification for this has ever been given.

Ten years previously, in the early 1960s, a Soviet defector called Anatoly Golitsyn had told MI5 that Wilson was a spy and that Hugh Gaitskell, Wilson's predecessor as Labour leader, had been assassinated to make way for him. The claim was rejected by MI5's director general – but it was probably believed by Angleton.

In 1974 sudden troop movements supported by tanks around Heathrow Airport were explained as a routine exercise to plan against a possible terrorist attack, but it was claimed by Wilson's private office that the prime minister was not warned of this in advance. Baroness Falkender, the former Marcia Williams, Wilson's most trusted aide, said she and the prime minister had both believed that the Army training exercise at Heathrow Airport was in reality either a show of strength or a training exercise for a coup.

The coup, which obviously never happened, was reportedly the brainchild of *Daily Mirror* publisher Lord Cecil King who allegedly attempted to recruit Lord Louis Mountbatten, the Queen's uncle, to lead the uprising. No proof for this extraordinary claim has ever been forthcoming, although the allegation was recently given fresh legs to a television audience of millions through the Netflix series *The Crown*, detailing the story of the Royal Family through the 20th century. The way Netflix tells it, the Queen summoned Mountbatten and told him to stop being so stupid. Whether such a confrontation happened is open to question.

No doubt Netflix took its script from the author Andrew Lownie who explored the alleged coup attempt in his 2019 book, *The Mountbattens: Their Lives & Loves*, suggesting that it required the Queen's intervention in order to dissuade Lord Mountbatten from proceeding.

In the 1987 book, *Spycatcher*, author Peter Wright claimed that "up to 30" MI5 officers joined a secret campaign to undermine Wilson in the hope that Lord Mountbatten would replace him. However, in Wright's book, it is claimed that Mountbatten refused as he saw this as treason.

Whatever the truth or otherwise of this, it is generally accepted by historians that the security services did take more than a passing interest in Harold Wilson's early career and were particularly keen to look into many visits the Labour leader made to the Soviet bloc in the 1950s.

Lord Hunt, who was Cabinet Secretary between 1973 and 1979, conducted an inquiry into Wilson's concerns that MI5 was bugging the Prime Minister's office. He concluded that "a few, a very few, malcontents in MI5" had "spread damaging malicious stories".

The producers of a BBC documentary 'Plot against Harold Wilson' confirmed that Hunt had admitted to them that the secret service was indeed taking steps against Wilson's government, but he refused to accept the idea of a coup, claiming that MI5 were acting under the suspicion that Wilson was a Soviet spy.

It is undeniable that tensions were running at fever pitch in the early 1980s. Margaret Thatcher was mid-way through her first term in office and her economic policies were forcing unprofitable industries to close with the Midland manufacturing base in particular facing decimation. Unemployment was soaring – up to 20 per cent in Coventry, for example, where an extraordinary 26,000 jobs disappeared in one month during the early 1980s – and a new era of wildcat strikes and trade union militancy began to sweep through factories.

Across the country almost three million were out of work by Christmas 1981 and there were riots in Brixton earlier that year. The workers were angry and their insecurity was starting to manifest itself on the shop floor. Margaret Thatcher's typically strident response was to describe striking miners as "the enemy within" and to abolish the Labour-led metropolitan county councils, including the Greater London Council, led by Ken Livingstone, which infuriated the prime minister by displaying a huge banner announcing the latest unemployment figures across the front of County Hall.

Thatcher became Tory leader off the back of Ted Heath's disastrous 1970-1974 government which presided over four years of industrial strife, with the government forced to ration power and impose a three-day week in response to strikes by miners. There then followed five years of ineffective Labour government under Wilson and then James Callaghan, where the top rate of tax on unearned income hit an eye-watering 98 per cent, culminating in what became known as the Winter of Discontent where even the dead went unburied because of strike action by public sector unions. With Labour under the leadership of Michael Foot from 1980 and increasingly influenced by the hard-left Militant, I suppose it is possible the British establishment may have been concerned enough about what might have happened were Thatcher to lose the 1983 general election to unleash the dark arts of MI5 on a regional political journalist.

My friend at the pub wasn't a member of the security services but he certainly knew highly-placed people who were. I didn't take him up on his suggestion that I should hand over information and the matter was never mentioned again.

When it comes to espionage Oxford is no match for Cambridge University, where the Philby, Burgess and Maclean spy ring, plus fourth and fifth men, passed secrets to the Soviet Union in the 1950s and 1960s. But Oxford did have a tenuous link to spying scandals as it was the home of Adrian Hollis, only son of Sir Roger Hollis, a former head of MI5 who after his death was accused of being Britain's greatest ever spy and a Soviet mole. In the early 1980s several books named Roger Hollis as a spy – a claim steadfastly denied by MI5 to this day – and an excited *Oxford Mail* news desk ordered me to 'doorstep' Adrian Hollis at his comfortable north Oxford villa. I recall Hollis junior emerging eventually to tell waiting reporters that he had nothing to say about allegations concerning his father, which of course made front-page headlines in the *Oxford Mail* and kept the story going.

Officially, the *Oxford Mail* and *Oxford Times* took an independent view of party politics and judged each issue on its merits before deciding on an editorial stance. I cannot recall, however, the *Oxford Times* ever publishing anything remotely supportive of Labour-controlled Oxford city council. Tony Price made little secret of his leanings towards the Conservative cause although he never prevailed upon me to give any particular slant to a news story.

Comment columns in the *Oxford Times* and the leader column, often written by me, were a different matter with the paper maintaining a rigorous right-of-centre stance which was generally supportive of Margaret Thatcher and her government and highly critical of Michael Foot and Labour. This suited me, for although I'd been a Labour voter as a young man I'd drifted away from the party following the Winter of Discontent and its drift ever-leftwards. While not a natural Tory, I backed Thatcher's move to sell off inefficient nationalised industries, and in particular the sale of council houses which, much to Labour's horror, allowed working class people to buy and inherit property and produced the greatest redistribution of wealth in British history.

The paper also took every opportunity to slam Oxford city council's supposed financial profligacy, in particular the decision in 1984 to build an ice rink at a cost of £2.5 million which became something of a cause célèbre in the newspaper's letters page. The *Oxford Times* took the view that if there were public demand for an ice rink, which it thought doubtful, then the private sector could and should meet that demand rather than the public purse. But the council pressed ahead and built the ice rink which is still in business today.

Price found himself in a difficult position in 1983 when the Conservative government, which he supported, decided to extend the M40 motorway from Great Milton just outside Oxford to Birmingham. The proposed route would cut through the ancient wetlands of Otmoor where the grid-like pattern of hedges and ditches is said to have been the landscape that inspired Lewis Carroll to devise the chessboard in Alice in Wonderland.

Price, who lived in a picture postcard thatched cottage at Stanton-St-John on the edge of Otmoor and clearly had a personal interest in getting the route changed, mobilised the *Oxford Times*'s and Oxford University's considerable influence at Government level. A vociferous protest campaign saw Friends of the Earth buy a plot of land on Otmoor, which they named Alice's Meadow, and sold it off piece by piece to 3,500 people in an effort to frustrate any attempts at compulsory purchase. The *Oxford Times* was very careful to make it clear it did not oppose the need for the M40 to be extended to deliver a better road link between London, Oxford and Birmingham, but simply wanted the route changed to avoid Otmoor. The campaign soon had the desired effect with the Department for Transport and plans for the road were swiftly re-drawn to incorporate a circuitous and expensive detour around the edge of Otmoor.

Chapter Thirteen

1983 General Election

The election was held on June 9, two months after I married my wife, Claire. We'd bought a small modern terraced house in Witney, about nine miles to the west of Oxford, for £20,000, which seemed like a colossal sum of money. The mortgage was arranged via an Oxford building society manager, who was also a Tory city councillor, who had delivered several speeches in the chamber describing just how easy it was for first-time buyers to obtain a mortgage without any need for a ten percent deposit. I challenged him to do just that, and unsurprisingly, for me, the process turned out to be very quick and simple.

I recall vividly my pride in being handed the keys and realising I'd finally got my feet on the bottom rung of the property ladder. We were to move again a couple of years later to a larger property just down the road which we bought for £40,000, the figure representing the impact on the housing market of galloping inflation at that time.

During the 1983 General Election campaign the Labour leader Michael Foot attracted large crowds of enthusiastic supporters wherever he went to speak, particularly younger people, just as Jeremy Corbyn would do years later during the 2017 and 2019 General Election campaigns. Meetings were sold out across the country, which was no mean feat at a time when the instant communication of the internet and social media did not exist.

I reported Foot's speech shortly before polling day to a rapturous crowd at a packed Oxford Town Hall with many locked outside unable to gain access where he accused Tory grandee Lord Hailsham of "licking Hitler's jackboots" at the infamous 1938 Munich by-election in Oxford by backing the Tory prime minister Neville Chamberlain and therefore supporting the appeasement of Hitler. Foot, it should be noted, was one of three authors of a polemical book called 'The Guilty Men', published in 1940 which attacked the British establishment for its failure to re-arm in the 1930s and for supporting the appeasement of Hitler. Some 43 years later, although the rest of the country had moved on, Foot was still fighting the issues of the 1930s. The slur against Hailsham drew massive applause from the town hall audience and prompted national newspaper headlines, but it seems highly unlikely that the events of the 1930s made much impact on the electorate in 1983, even in somewhere as idiosyncratic as Oxford.

I followed camera crews and Foot around Banbury Market in a chaotic walkabout where he issued an impromptu pledge to scrap NHS prescription charges, the imposition of which for dental care and spectacles led to Labour's Bevanite split in the 1950s. The very fact that Labour saw fit to waste time campaigning in such a rock-solid safe Tory seat as Banbury was, in my view, a fair indication of the party's state of denial under Foot's leadership.

These were days when leading politicians actually met real people as opposed to party stooges, and anything could happen as a result. In this case, a shopper asked Foot to his face what he would do about prescription charges were he to be prime minister. "They will have to go," came the reply. What the national journalists covering the walkabout conveniently did not mention in their reports, however, was the caveat Foot applied to his remarks: "We won't be able to afford to do it straight away of course." As far as the next day's *Daily Telegraph* and *Daily Mail* were concerned, Foot had committed taxpayers to finding billions of pounds to scrap prescription charges and the money needed to do that could only be generated in one way – by increasing taxes.

Two new parliamentary seats were created in Oxford for the 1983 General Election. Both went to Conservative candidates, Oxford West and Abingdon being won by John Patten and Oxford East by Steven Norris. Patten's main rival was Evan Luard, a former Labour MP for Oxford who stood as a candidate for the newly-formed Social Democratic Party. Luard came second with a respectable 33 percent of the votes, pushing left-wing Labour candidate and BBC producer Julian Jacottet into third place.

The founding of the SDP on March 26 1981 by four senior Labour party MPs, Roy Jenkins, Dr David Owen, Bill Rogers and Shirley Williams, proved to be an interesting interlude for the Oxford Times, chiefly because Evan Luard became one of the first former Labour MPs to join the new party and signal his intention to stand in Oxford West and Abingdon at the next General Election.

I attended a press conference at Luard's home in Oxford, with David Owen also present, where the modernising credentials of the SDP were spelt out. It would even be possible, Owen announced, to join the new party simply by telephoning with a credit or debit card number, something that came across as excitingly cutting-edge at the time.

For a brief moment the SDP's popularity was so great that the prospects of a second victory for Margaret Thatcher at the next election were questionable, at least that's the way it felt at the time. It appeared perfectly possible that the SDP really was on course to deliver what it claimed to be able to achieve – break the mould of British politics by forming an electable left of centre social democratic party along European lines. Such an outcome would not have been to the liking of the *Oxford Times* which regarded the SDP and the Liberals with thinly disguised disdain.

In the event, it was a damned close-run thing. At the 1983 General Election the SDP-Liberal Alliance won 25 percent of the national vote compared to Labour's disastrous 28 percent, the party's worst performance since 1918, and 44 percent for the Conservatives with Mrs Thatcher no doubt helped by the jingoistic 'Falklands Factor' – a boost in Tory support following the bloody conflict in the South Atlantic. Ultimately, Britain's first past the post electoral system dashed the hopes of both the SDP and the Liberals and the two parties ended up with only 23 Alliance MPs. The unfairness of the system can be seen starkly by the fact that Labour, polling only three percent nationally more than the SDP, ended up with 209 seats, eight times as many as the Alliance.

Patten and Norris were markedly different characters and a friendly rivalry existed between them. Patten, a Roman Catholic educated by Jesuits at Wimbledon College, was a graduate of Sidney Sussex College, Cambridge. Norris had a rather more down to earth upbringing and attended the Liverpool Institute at the same time as George Harrison, from where he managed to win an open exhibition to Worcester College, Oxford. After university he pursued a career in the motor industry and engineering before entering politics. Patten was bookish, or at least gave the impression of being so, while Norris was a Scouser who, most unusually for a Tory MP, had worked in car factories.

Norris had an easy relationship with journalists. Patten was rather more difficult and appeared to regard himself as a highly important figure in Oxford. Bouffant hair and dressed like a dandy, he would strut around the city and had the annoying habit of demanding a journalist read back to him the notes taken during an interview, which I did only once before telling him to stop messing about. His nickname on the *Oxford Times* news desk was 'the vicar of Bray' after the 18th century satirical song depicting the contortions of principle gone through by a clergyman who constantly changed his beliefs to suit the times.

Norris is probably best remembered for his failed attempt to become mayor of London, losing to Ken Livingstone, and for unfortunate publicity surrounding his personal life which led to *Private Eye* dubbing him 'Shagger Norris'. Patten, meanwhile, served as Secretary of State for Education from 1992 to 1994 where he ended up on the wrong end of legal action by the highly-regarded Birmingham chief education officer Tim Brighouse, who he had most unwisely described as "a madman …. wandering the streets, frightening the children". Brighouse, who had previously crossed swords with Patten when he was chief education officer at Oxfordshire County Council from 1978 to 1989, sued and won substantial damages which were donated to educational charities helping to set up the University of the First Age.

Patten and Norris were in the habit of throwing a joint drinks party for the media at Christmas. This much sought-after event was generally held at Hertford College and was unusual because only one alcoholic drink was available – White Lady cocktails, an amalgamation of gin, Cointreau, lemon juice and egg white shaken and served ice cold. We'd arrive there after a few beers at the nearby Turf Tavern, famous in Oxford mythology as the pub where Thomas Hardy's *Jude the Obscure* recited the Apostles' Creed in Latin in a failed attempt to prove himself worthy of admission to the University, and then consume as many White Ladies as possible in the hour or so allotted for Patten and Norris's cocktail party.

The stewards at Hertford could certainly fix a mean White Lady, as many Oxford journalists would be able to confirm once they had sobered up. One year, Norris asked for the event to be switched to Worcester College, where he had studied, and vowed privately to make the party the best ever. Sadly, the Worcester bar staff were either not so well versed in mixing White Ladies as their compatriots at Hertford, or more likely had under-estimated the ability of journalists to consume said cocktail at rapid pace. In no time at all the pre-prepared cocktails had disappeared down the throats of the thirsty hacks and the mixing of replacements proved a fastidious and messy job. Soon the bar was awash with egg shells and yolks, much to the amusement of Patten and the annoyance of Norris.

Chapter Fourteen

Marathon Council Meetings

I t was obvious when I arrived at Oxford that the *Mail* and *Times* shared news desk was going to be far more hands-on than had been the case in Reading, where day to day supervision of reporters was lax to say the least. It was made clear to all reporters that, when out of the office, they must check in with news editors by telephone every 30 minutes or so. I easily swerved around the rules by explaining that it would be inadvisable to keep leaving council committee meetings to phone the office. I might miss a good story. The excuse seemed to be accepted.

The closest pub to the *Oxford Mail* and *Times* offices on the Osney Mead industrial estate was the Waterman's Arms, an old and at that time rather run-down Victorian boozer by the Thames and no more than a five-minute walk away. Further afield in North Hinksey, The Fishes, a pleasant 20-minute stroll along a bridleway, was an alternative location and the daily drinking venue for *Oxford Mail* deputy editor Colin Dobson and his pals.

Drinking habits on the *Oxford Mail* and *Times* were conducted at a far more conservative pace than had been the case in Reading, and for a very good reason since the pressures of providing enough news to fill both a daily and a weekly paper were such that anyone risking four or five pints in the middle of the day would soon have been found out, taken to one side and told to stop. That's not to say there wasn't party-time most evenings, but by 1983 I was married and heading straight home each night to my wife rather than joining work colleagues in the pub.

The more cerebral reporters and subs sipped wine rather than beer, which was quite unusual in 1980, and lunchtimes were often spent huddled around a table at the Waterman's attempting to solve *The Times* crossword.

Editorial perks at the *Oxford Mail* and *Times* were occasionally of a superior level. Having returned from lunch one day I became aware that the news desk was trying to offload VIP tickets for a match at the Kirtlington Polo Club, and as the tickets stated that HRH the Prince of Wales was to be the principal guest I felt the chance to mingle with royalty was too good to turn down.

Claire and I duly turned up at the club dressed in our Sunday best, to be ushered into a roped-off VIP area and handed glasses of Krug champagne from the sponsors who seemed ridiculously grateful that the *Oxford Times* was taking an interest in their event. A grey Aston Martin roared into the car park with the Prince behind the wheel, but there was no sign of Lady Diana Spencer to whom he had recently become engaged. Astonishingly, in the days when the royal family were not as closely protected as is the case now, we were allowed into the VIP area simply by producing our tickets with no need to prove identity and no security checks. I could have been carrying a gun, knife or bomb for all anyone knew. In the event I was armed only with a notebook and pen.

One of the more unusual things about the *Oxford Mail* and *Times* was that the newspapers' owners, Westminster Press, and the two editors, raised no objection to a busy freelance news operation run by the *Mail* and *Times* news editor who would sell any decent story to national newspapers as soon as it had appeared in the Oxford papers. This was a highly lucrative business particularly since titles such as the *Daily Mail*, *Daily Telegraph*, *Guardian* and *Times* would snap up almost any story from Oxford, particularly if the University was involved.

Reporters who had written stories that had been sold-on would receive a cheque once a month representing their share of the booty, which could easily amount to half a week's wages or more. An obvious question arose: why didn't the newspapers take control of this lucrative sideshow, and pocket the money since all of the stories sold had been written by *Mail* and *Times* journalists and were therefore the property of Westminster Press? And how on earth did the news editor, the loveliest and gentlest of men who cycled to Oxford Prison to play the organ at church services for inmates on Sundays for 30 years, ever have the time to run a news agency as well as overseeing the *Mail* and *Times* news operation?

One of the larger payments I received from the freelance agency concerned a story about an Oxfordshire teacher who showed children in her care the X-rated video *The Texas Chainsaw Massacre*. When the county council attempted to dismiss her, the teacher unwisely went to an employment tribunal which I covered for the *Oxford Mail*. The story was sold to the *Sun* newspaper, where it was splashed across the front page.

I arrived at Oxford shortly after the Conservatives lost control of the city council to Labour, bringing four years of Tory rule to an end. Labour would be in charge for the next 20 years. By 2000, the Conservatives were down to one member, and since 2001 Oxford City Council has been a Tory-free zone marking an extraordinary turnaround in the space of two decades.

City council meetings were held at the splendid Victorian Town Hall in St Aldate's, up the road from Christ Church, and were typically a microcosm of an Oxford University debating society with the most fury and spleen reserved for pointless debates on matters over which the council had no control whatsoever – fox hunting, for example, numerous aspects of national Government policy, and the need to demonstrate socialist solidarity by purchasing Nicaraguan coffee for the Town Hall, which was duly bought but tasted foul. Naturally, the coffee saga and attempts to ban foxhunting on council-owned land attracted the wrath of the *Oxford Times* which condemned the move as tantamount to class war.

Full council meetings began at 2.30pm and sometimes continued until midnight or gone, although during the hours of 5.30 to 10 plenty of council members and the media spent more time setting the world to rights in in the Old Tom pub over the road than they ever did in the council chamber. For the first time in my career, I didn't mind the long hours as the *Oxford Mail* and *Times* allowed reporters to log the time they worked and awarded days off when contracted hours had been exceeded, a refreshing change from Reading where no such arrangement existed.

Long and vindictive rows about planning applications were a staple diet in Oxford where it seemed that almost any proposal to build something new attracted opposition from the university or environmental action groups, whipped up by the *Oxford Times*'s general suspicion of change. A proposal to redevelop Oxford's squalid Gloucester Green coach station dragged on for more than a year, and the London-based developers behind the scheme did not shy away from using what might today be considered questionable methods to court the local media. The firm had a VIP box at Tottenham Hotspur's White Hart Lane ground to which I was invited for a memorably boozy lunch. But if the developers thought their hospitality would lead to positive coverage in the *Oxford Mail* and *Oxford Times*, they were wrong for I'd consumed so much champagne and brandy by the end of the day that I could hardly remember the match score let alone the finer details of the Gloucester Green development.

Oxfordshire County Council had been controlled by the Conservatives ever since party politics gained a toehold in local government, but the Tories were forced to form a minority administration following the 1985 elections as no political party had an overall majority.

In 1980 there were still half a dozen or so Independent members of the council, although they were Tories in all but name, representing the most rural parts of the county mainly in the Vale of White Horse district. The council had more than its fair share of eccentrics and one of the Independent members, a farmer, famously declared there should be no need at all for councils to spend money on running refuse collection services as people could easily bury rubbish in their gardens. There again, he did have about 150 acres of farmland to dig holes in. Most of the Independents eventually joined the Conservatives where they did not take kindly to being whipped into line. One veteran former Independent turned Tory mounted a silent protest by sitting through the long county council meetings ostentatiously reading a coffee-table book of British horses only pausing to raise his hand to vote when required to do so.

Monthly meetings of Oxfordshire county council were notable for lavish lunches provided for council members and officers, to which the media were invited. A buffet was simply groaning with cold rare roast beef, salmon, and every conceivable type of salad, followed by a choice of puddings. Wine was plentiful and free of charge too, so it wasn't surprising when the meetings resumed at 2pm a few council members dozed quietly in the chamber while others became somewhat over-animated having consumed more alcohol than was good for them. As a result, afternoon sessions were rarely dull and always a tester for the chairman.

The meetings improved from my point of view during 1981-1982 when the redoubtable Olive Gibbs became county council chair. I'd struck up a close relationship with Olive, a veteran Oxford Labour councillor, friend of Michael Foot, and a founder member and former chair of the Campaign for Nuclear Disarmament, who was in her second stint at the head of the county council having held the post before in 1974-1975. It was no secret that Olive liked the company of young male journalists, particularly those that, like her, were partial to a drink and to political gossip and we became firm friends.

The county council chairman benefited from an office at Shire Hall, an allowance for entertaining, and a well-stocked cocktail cabinet. Generally during the hour or so before the lunch break Olive would ask the vice-chairman to preside over the meeting and retire to her office. I would follow discreetly a few minutes later to discover the gin bottle open and two glasses at the ready. Olive would proceed to lambast the county council, the city council and Oxford in general, usually reserved her most scathing comments for fellow Labour politicians who had crossed her or whose views she did not care for. She particularly disliked sanctimonious do-gooders, hair-shirt socialists, left-wing vicars, and reserved special wrath for teetotalers who she didn't understand at all and viewed with the utmost suspicion.

One area upon which we felt obliged to agree to disagree was the thorny issue of nuclear weapons. Olive, as a former CND chair, believed Britain should follow the path of unilateral nuclear disarmament, a pledge that was duly approved by the 1960 and 1982 Labour party conferences, although overturned afterwards by the party leadership on both occasions. I took the view, fairly typically for a child of the cold war, that if the Soviets had nuclear weapons then so should we. In the end, we called a truce and avoided nuclear talk to concentrate instead on a stiff gin and tonic.

Olive was fascinated to discover that I had read the *Oxford Times*'s pre-prepared obituary for use after her death and spent a long time unsuccessfully attempting to convince me she really ought to be able to read the wording to make sure the biographical details were correct. The obit had been written by a former *Oxford Times* news editor whom Olive denounced as "a terrible old Tory" and she was convinced he would take the opportunity to condemn her from beyond the grave. In fact, apart from correctly describing her as a "stormy petrel", the obituary was entirely fair and suitably appreciative of one of Oxford's post-war political giants.

As well as entertaining in her county council office, Olive presided over what amounted to an 'Oxford salon' at her Iffley Road home where a wide selection of politicians and 'interesting' people could regularly be found discussing issues of the day over lethal gin and tonics. She had plenty of enemies in the local Labour party, though, where some rather unfairly derided her as nothing more than a latter-day 'Queen Elizabeth I' with her sycophantic followers paying homage by bowing and scraping at court.

Chapter Fifteen

Robert Maxwell

The tycoon Robert Maxwell was a bombastic bully who will largely be remembered for building a huge publishing empire and fleecing *Daily Mirror* pension funds of hundreds of millions of pounds – a crime only uncovered following his death in 1991 when he drowned after falling overboard in mysterious circumstances from his luxury yacht off the coast of Tenerife.

Maxwell was a prominent Labour party member and a former MP for Buckingham who lived at Headington Hill Hall in Oxford, which was owned by the city council. Maxwell managed to negotiate a peppercorn rent for the mansion, which was built in 1824 for the Morrell family of local brewers. He liked to refer to the property as 'the best council house in the country', a jibe designed to infuriate local Labour politicians, which it certainly did.

There weren't many Labour councillors who had anything good to say about Maxwell. He was a thorn in the flesh of the Oxford Labour party and was someone of whom the city council was always wary. There were tales of hostility to trade unions at the companies he controlled, most notably the Oxford-based Pergamon Press publishing house. Members of the local party attempted on several occasions to have Maxwell disciplined or his Labour membership revoked, citing alleged ill treatment of trade unionists, but they were unsuccessful.

As repulsive as Maxwell may have been, he had plenty of allies in the national party at the top of Labour's ranks who were prepared to turn a blind eye to his shortcomings even though his business record was tarnished. Some 20 years before he died a Department of Trade and Industry inquiry into allegations about the profitability of Pergamon Press concluded that "Robert Maxwell is not a person who can be relied upon to exercise proper stewardship of a publicly quoted company". The inquiry, which effectively dashed his attempts to buy the *News of the World*, found that Maxwell had contrived to maximise Pergamon's share price through transactions between his private family companies.

Oxford City Council found itself embarrassed in 1983 upon the occasion of Maxwell's 60th birthday. A lavish party at Headington Hill Hall attended by civic leaders, national politicians, and celebrities culminated in a lengthy and extremely loud firework display. The good people of Oxford were not amused at rockets raining down on them in the early hours and numerous complaints were lodged with the council's environmental health department, but predictably enough no action was ever taken.

I met Maxwell only twice, once at a press conference he gave in London to launch the *Daily Mirror*'s £1 million bingo game, and secondly in 1983 to conduct an interview about his odd plan to amalgamate Reading Football Club and Oxford United FC to form a new club to be called the Thames Valley Royals.

The *Oxford Mail* found out about the bingo press conference only a couple of hours before it was due to begin. Terry Page asked me to drop everything, drive to the *Mirror*'s Holborn headquarters in central London, and attend the press briefing. He also gave me a chit for £20, which I exchanged at the *Mail*'s accounts department on the way out, adding: "You'll need some money if you're going to London. Just make sure you get receipts." Twenty pounds in 1983 would be worth about £70 now and the idea that a regional newspaper reporter would be casually handed such a sum by his editor today is laughable. Naturally, I spent the money on a decent lunch and returned to Oxford, fully armed with receipts.

Maxwell's idea for the Thames Valley Royals was that the new team would play in a purpose-built stadium on a site to be identified, but until a ground could be built the Royals would play matches alternately at each other's grounds in Oxford and Reading. In putting forward his proposal Maxwell, who was the Oxford United chairman, demonstrated scant knowledge of footballing tribalism. As anyone could have told him, and perhaps did tell him for all I knew, Oxford and Reading were then and remain so today the deadliest of rivals whose supporters would rather have knocked six-inch nails into their knee caps than countenance a merger.

The plan prompted a storm in the local media. One angry Oxford fan wrote to the *Oxford Mail*: "I would not follow Thames Valley Royals or whatever their name is if they played at the end of my street". For his part the chairman of the Reading Supporters Club, said: "Our fans can't stand Oxford fans and I can't see them travelling to Oxford to watch the new team."

The scheme duly fell apart following massive protests from supporters of both clubs and, in typical shady Maxwellian fashion, there were legal implications leading to a successful challenge in the High Court by a Reading director to the sale of some of the club's shares, effectively putting paid to any merger.

Days before the collapse of the scheme the *Oxford Mail* received a summons from Maxwell and I was dispatched to Headington Hall to capture his thoughts about Thames Valley Royals. I was shown into Maxwell's office which was about the size of a tennis court and featured the largest boardroom table I have ever seen. The huge figure of Maxwell sat at the head of the table. Naturally, I went to sit next to him but he waved a chubby hand indicating a spot about six seats away instead. It didn't matter where in the room I was sitting for it quickly became obvious I was there to listen and take dictation from him, and certainly not to ask questions.

Maxwell began: "You will say, Mr Robert Maxwell, chairman of Oxford United Football Club, said today that the proposed merger with Reading Football Club …" And he went on and on embellishing the supposed advantages of a merger, interrupted by regular telephone calls which necessitated Maxwell barking orders down the line about buying and selling various shares. I was unsure whether the calls were genuine, or staged to impress me. Either way, it was probably the only 'interview' in my career where I didn't get to ask a single question before being shown out of the door.

Chapter Sixteen

The Frewen Club

Half-way down St Aldate's, opposite Christ Church and close to the Old Tom pub, is a highly-polished green door at number 98 with nothing to indicate what lies behind. For those in the know, this is the Frewen Club, one of Oxford's oldest gentlemen's institutions where I was proud to be a member from 1982 to 1988.

This is a club with history. It was formed in 1869 by officers and non-commissioned officers of the 2nd Oxfordshire Rifle Volunteer Corps, "to further comradeship among the volunteers and to encourage relationships with the townspeople". Then known as the 2nd Oxfordshire Rifle Volunteer Corps Club, it occupied rooms at the Three Cups Hotel in Queen Street and then at unknown premises in Cornmarket Street before moving in 1876 to 98 St Aldate's, becoming the Frewen Club in 1888.

When I joined the Frewen Club it gave every impression of being stuck firmly in the England of a bygone age. It was the type of institution that people who had attended minor public schools probably thought resembled a smart London club. On the plus side, it was a safe haven for businessmen who wanted to relax, drink and eat, well away from the forbidding glare of their wives or girlfriends. P G Wodehouse's Bertie Wooster, who spent many hours avoiding his overbearing aunts by idling his life away at the fictional Drones Club in London, would instantly have been at home at the Frewen among like-minded chums, as in fact would Dickens's Mr Pickwick and his friends a century earlier.

A narrow building on several floors, the Frewen Club consisted of two bar areas with well-worn leather armchairs and comfy sofas, a dining room dominated by a large refectory-type table, a fine snooker room on the top floor, and accommodation for Tom Curtin and his wife Marjorie who were the stewards when I was a member. Tom, who retained expert knowledge of the club's long history, liked to tell new members how stewards between the two world wars were issued with felt slippers by the management committee lest their footsteps on the polished wooden floorboards disturb slumbering members. Those were the days.

There were certain standards to be upheld at all costs. I never once heard Tom refer to a member by his first name. It was always 'Sir' or 'Mr Dale'. There was a club tie and a club bow tie, a strict dress code demanding jackets and ties be worn at all times, apart from the hottest of summer days when the 'committee' might relax the dress code and allow jackets to be removed. No women were permitted to be members or enter the premises, except for Mrs Curtin, although she was only ever seen supervising the dining room and never behind the bar. It was claimed several years before I joined that the club committee decided to place black-out curtains across the snooker room windows after a lady sitting on the top deck of a bus passing along St Aldate's glanced up and was astonished to see her husband wielding a cue. She had no idea that her other half was a member of the club, let alone played snooker, when in her view he should have been working.

The club rules were sacrosanct. Under no circumstances could a guest of a member buy drinks. A large chair in the corner of the bar was for the club President and any member caught sitting in the chair when the President entered the room would be the subject of hoots of laughter and 'fined' for the misdemeanour, requiring them to buy a drink for everyone present in the club at the time.

On the bar was placed an ancient leather-coated notebook in which members were able to strike wagers against each other. For example, 'Mr Heath bets Mr Parsons that Cambridge will win the University Boat Race by more than three lengths. The loser to provide the winner with a case of decent claret'. Each bet would be solemnly witnessed by two members, and wagers were expected to be paid in full and promptly.

There were special Frewen Club occasions such as a coach trip to Ladies' Day at Royal Ascot when members' wives and girlfriends would be treated to a day at the races. The annual Frewen golf competition was staged at the splendid Frilford Heath course. Conker Night took place in October, a noisy and drunken occasion when members would compete for a silver cup. All of the conkers used in the competition had to be solemnly authenticated by the committee as untreated to avoid sneaky Frewenites attempting to gain an unfair advantage by baking or soaking their own conkers in vinegar, a trick that was supposed to toughen the skin.

Punch Night at Christmas was one occasion when the ladies did get involved, albeit on the sidelines. They were invited to bake mince pies and then to serenade the men from the balcony overlooking Trinity College's dining room with carols as the Frewen members proceeded to pour as much of a lethal whisky-based punch based on a 19th century recipe down their necks as they could manage without falling over.

Frewen Club lunches, which took place Monday to Friday, were legendary for two things: nursery food and excessive drinking. Mrs Curtin's culinary skills were fine as far as they went, but didn't extend much beyond shepherd's pie, pork chops, and gammon and pineapple with peas and mashed potato, and the portions weren't exactly large. A few members were in the habit of grumbling about the lack of gastronomic appeal and demanded improvements to the menu, but the Frewen Club was the sort of place where the pace of change was glacial, and the menu was not altered during my time as a member.

Reservations for places at the long dining table, which sat about 20 people, were always competitive so if you required lunch it was a case of telephoning first thing in the morning. An unwritten club convention stated that every member attending a lunch was expected to buy a bottle of wine, so a full table involved much alcohol, with predictable results for anyone intending to work in the afternoon. The Burns' Day lunch held every January to celebrate the great Scottish poet was a particularly boozy and popular occasion with Frewen Club members and guests taking full advantage of bottles of whisky passed around the table as the haggis was piped in and afternoons were wiped out.

Members without the time or inclination to take a formal lunch could buy sandwiches at the bar – anything you want as long as it's ham or beef. Buying a beef sandwich involved making a tricky decision about 'Mr Aubrey's horseradish sauce'. This was a lethal home-made concoction supplied by a club member sourced from horseradish dug from the Oxfordshire hedgerows the use of which always prompted a grave health warning from the Steward: "Would you like some of Mr Aubrey's horseradish, Sir? Some members do find it a little hot though, Sir."

The changing of the club's wine list, which took place every few years, was another much-anticipated occasion where wine merchants were invited to bring in free samples of their merchandise for a members' wine-tasting evening. The concept of spitting the wine out after tasting was certainly not something that appealed to Frewen Club members, which resulted in fairly predictable repercussions of drunkenness after an hour or so.

As might be expected of such a venerable institution, the Frewen Club had plenty of colourful characters among its membership and the use of fairly obvious nicknames was commonplace. An Oxford professor of Biology, Dr Ken Lewis, a mean snooker player whose voice boomed across the club because he was stone deaf, was always referred to as 'The Doctor'. Ken appointed himself to keep a friendly eye on new Frewenites and would bellow 'new member, new member' at the top of his voice when a strange face entered the club. Another member who kept a boat at Hamble on the south coast was known as 'The Admiral'. And an outspoken local solicitor was known to all as 'The Beast'.

The Beast adopted a peculiarly-exaggerated rural Oxfordshire accent, with weird mannerisms in his speech. When ordering a ham sandwich for lunch. He'd say: "I'll 'ave 'arry 'ammers Tom, arrgh, 'arry 'ammers, arrgh, that's what I'll 'ave, Tom." No one seemed to think this the least bit unusual, or kept their thoughts to themselves if they did. After a few pints of beer, he'd amuse members with tales of his experiences at the local magistrates' court, in particular his success in obtaining a not guilty verdict for a businessman charged with committing gross indecency in a public toilet. "I said to the chairman of the bench, 'my client, he was just shaking the end of it to get the last drops off, arrgh, that's what 'e was doing, arrgh, just shaking it, 'e weren't doing nothing else your worships."

The Frewen Club was an obvious bolt hole for me as it is situated about 50 yards from the Town Hall steps. When a council committee meeting became too boring, which was a common occurrence, I'd nip over the road for a quick pint and use the club's phone booth to put over copy to the news desk. It was also a great place for finding out what was going on in the city's business world since most of the members were professional people, typically lawyers, even a high court judge, as well as accountants, company directors and business owners and a fair smattering of academics from the University. There were very few members from the media since journalists were not regarded as the type of people likely to turn a blind eye to the club's misogynistic tendencies, and indeed the *Oxford Mail* had already published stories questioning whether there was any longer a place in modern society for a men-only club and hinting that applicants from an ethnic minority background were being denied membership.

In 1998 the *Oxford Mail* took aim at the club, describing Frewenites as the sort of people "who dreamt of the days when Britannia ruled the waves and the roast beef of olde England came without a health warning". Yet, 22 years later, the Frewen Club is still there and recently celebrated its 150th birthday. It still only admits men and has more than 350 members including judges, barristers, bankers and many others from the top tranche of the Oxford business community.

I had no direct knowledge of discrimination on the grounds of race, although the membership was wholly white during my time. It was certainly very difficult to become a member and the club ran a vetting system to make sure applicants were 'the right sort of chap. This involved bringing someone wishing to join to the club for a drink and for lunch at least four or five times, where the prospective newcomer would be quietly assessed by members. Ultimately, the club's management committee had the final say over who could and could not become a member and operated a 'black ball' system which meant applicants had to be approved by the entire committee.

Somehow, I got in at the first time of asking, and so too did the Labour leader of Oxford City Council, Albert Ramsay, who was an enthusiastic Frewen member often to be found at lunchtime enjoying a beer and taking full advantage of the club protocol that politics was a frowned-upon topic of conversation. It seems unlikely now that a Labour council leader would get away with membership of a men-only drinking club where most members held views well to the right of centre, but you never know.

Chapter Seventeen

Supermac and Mrs Thatcher

One of the more unusual things I was asked to do at the *Oxford Mail* and *Times* was to try to contact the former prime minister Harold Macmillan, by now the Earl of Stockton, who at the age of 91 had launched a thinly-veiled attack on Mrs Thatcher's government in a speech to the Tory Reform Group. His comments in 1985, a year before he died, were interpreted as criticism of her privatisation policy which he likened mischievously to a stately home owner flogging the family silver: "The sale of assets is common with individuals and states when they run into financial difficulties. First, all the Georgian silver goes, and then all that nice furniture that used to be in the saloon. Then the Canalettos go."

Macmillan was Chancellor of Oxford University so his comments were of interest to the Oxford media and it so happened through the *Oxford Times*'s university contacts we were able to obtain a telephone number for Birch Grove, Macmillan's Sussex mansion. I dialled the number, not expecting for a moment any success, but the phone was picked up at the other end and a quavering, unmistakably plummy voice, said: "Hello ... who is this?" I asked whether I was talking to the Earl of Stockton and explained I was from the *Oxford Times* seeking an interview about his recent comments regarding the government. The cut-glass tone changed immediately to be replaced by a cackle and what can only be described as the worst cockney accent since Dick Van Dyke in the film Mary Poppins: "No Sir, 'e ain't 'ere." The telephone at Birch Grove was firmly put down. Could it have been Macmillan? I'm convinced it was.

If Macmillan's intervention wasn't embarrassing enough, worse was to follow for the Government when academics at Oxford University took revenge by refusing to grant an honorary degree to Margaret Thatcher, making her the first and, so far, only British prime minister to be so snubbed. University Dons lobbied for refusal in protest against government cuts to higher education spending, and the campaign quickly gained traction and turned into an unprecedented Oxford establishment denunciation of Thatcherism.

All Dons and administrators at Oxford were permitted to vote and more than 1,000 queued in academic gowns at the entrance to the Sheldonian

Theatre to have their say, with the award finally being rejected by 738 to 319. Mrs Thatcher was to be denied the honour of wearing a scarlet and crimson gown and velvet bonnet of a doctor of civil law.

Tony Price was aghast at Oxford's treatment of the prime minister and predictably enough the *Oxford Times* argued loudly that grubby politics should not cloud people's minds and that as the country's first female prime minister Mrs Thatcher clearly deserved an honorary degree to complement the degree in chemistry she had already earned in 1947 at Somerville College, Oxford.

As if to underline a general rule in politics that the more meaningless something is the more interest there will be in it, media from across the globe, including the *Washington Post* and *New York Times*, flocked to Oxford to witness the humiliation of the prime minister. Foreign journalists turned up at the *Mail* and *Times* offices demanding to know "where is the university", to which the obvious answer was "it is all around you". The whole saga proved to be a very lucrative earner for the news editor's freelance operation, and for quite a few *Mail* and *Times* reporters as well.

Thousands of spectators baying for Mrs Thatcher's blood flocked to Broad Street and Catte Street jostling with television camera crews to witness proceedings and gasp in awe at Oxford's ability to put on a colourful show. Impromptu parties sprang up and every public house within a quarter of a mile was rammed full of anti-Thatcher revellers.

It was obvious from an early stage which way the vote was going to go, and it would not be in the prime minister's favour. The *Guardian* newspaper summed it up thus: "The 'No' exit of Sir Christopher Wren's Sheldonian Theatre was jammed like a London Tube station in the rush hour long after the 'Aye' door had taken its last voter."

It quickly became clear that the scale of the Prime Minister's defeat was due to a huge turnout by scientific and medical dons, who rarely take part in academic debates but were, it seemed, persuaded to make a stand by the effects of government spending cuts on their research.

The result was played down by Downing Street with a spokesman stating that Mrs Thatcher would be the last person in the world to want an honour if someone didn't wish to bestow it upon her. Her official biographer Charles Moore makes it clear that the prime minister received conflicting advice about the wisdom of allowing her name to go forward for consideration of an honorary degree. When she received the official invitation, she also got a letter from the Conservative historian Robert Blake, who was Provost of The Queen's College, Oxford. He said how delighted he was, and told her not to worry about the proviso that a vote on the matter might be taken in Congregation. "It is conceivable that some left-wing don might mount a challenge. I personally think it is very unlikely, but I might be wrong. I am confident, however, that if there were a vote, you would win it," Blake wrote, demonstrating how spectacularly out of touch he had become.

Mrs Thatcher's principal private secretary, Robin Butler, had his ear much closer to the ground. He wrote a note accompanying Blake's letter warning the prime minister that "left-wingers in the university will take the opportunity of running a campaign against you before the vote in Congregation".

Butler was correct and it was never again to be 'glad confident morning' for Mrs Thatcher in Oxford, for Blake in a colossal misjudgement had seriously underestimated the anti-Thatcher sentiment flowing through the university. Charles Moore explained why he believed the vote went the way it did: "Those who supported the honorary degree thought that the dons who voted it down were resentful of the loss of their privileged status in society as intellectuals automatically deferred to and subsidised by governments and saw Mrs Thatcher as a parvenue."

Moore also made what I think is a highly valid point, that the decision to deny the prime minister a great honour owed as much to snobbery as anything else. Mighty Oxford University never quite managed to get over the fact that a middle class Tory housewife from an unfashionable college like Somerville managed to beat all male contenders to become Britain's first female prime minister. As Moore puts it in the Thatcher memoirs: "What seems most strange in retrospect is how little prominence was given to the point about Mrs Thatcher being Oxford's own, and the first of her sex. One needs to imagine Harvard refusing an honorary degree to America's first black president Barack Obama (who attended Harvard Law School) because of disagreement with his education policies, to see how extraordinary the Oxford decision looks today – and looked even at the time – to the wider world."

Chapter Eighteen

New Responsibilities and a Scoop

T wo years after joining the *Oxford Mail* and *Times* I was invited by Page and Price to take on the additional responsibility of health correspondent, writing about the affairs of Oxford Regional Health Authority and Oxfordshire Health Authority as well as continuing to report on local government. The move made a lot of sense logistically because health authorities were moving sharply up the political agenda as the implications that spending cuts imposed by Margaret Thatcher's government were likely to have on hospitals and patient care began to hit home.

Oxford Regional Health Authority, the strategic body responsible for setting health policy across the region, was giving the impression of being trapped in a time warp, doing its best to ignore the direct implications for the NHS of the public spending squeeze. Its board was dominated by powerful and lofty medical consultants and clinicians who never before had to bother about keeping spending within budget. Journalists covering RHA meetings were invited to stay for jolly lunches with plentiful glasses of sherry and a superlative spread of cold meats and salads. The tradition of inviting the media ended abruptly, I am proud to say, after a string of my exclusive stories in the *Oxford Mail* and *Times* revealed the true extent of the health authority's parlous finances and the harmful impact spending cuts would have on patients. Inconvenient truths that the RHA would have preferred to keep behind closed doors could not be silenced by a free lunch.

Oxfordshire District Health Authority, the body responsible for delivering health services across the county, was similarly finding it difficult to cope with financially challenging times. Its chairman from 1981 to 1984 was Sir John Habakkuk, a somewhat short-tempered economics professor and Fellow of All Souls College, Oxford, who while undoubtedly being more than intellectually equipped to chair the health authority, had neither the patience nor the diplomatic skills required to deal with Socialist Workers Party and other far-left supporters who regularly demonstrated and even invaded meetings bringing proceedings to a halt to protest at spending cuts.

Shortly after taking over the health brief I was walking along Hythe Bridge Street on my way to Oxford town hall when I saw a Labour member of both the county council and the regional health authority cycling towards me. Stopping briefly, he thrust a hand into his bicycle basket, pulled out a wad of papers, and said "here you are, you'll find this interesting" before cycling off into the distance.

To describe the documents as interesting was something of an understatement. When I looked at the sheaf of papers he had handed me, I discovered my informant had leaked in its entirety a highly confidential draft Regional Health Authority plan that proposed to slash spending by £12 million – a substantial sum then and equivalent to about £45 million today. Closer examination confirmed that most of the savings proposed were so controversial and would probably have required Government approval anyway that they were most unlikely to happen. I never quite decided whether this was an example of the health authority's naivety, proposing unacceptable savings in a state of panic, or perhaps more likely a subtle ploy to put forward cuts that the medical profession knew were most unlikely to be approved and could therefore be replaced by financial savings more acceptable to politicians with the result that everyone would breathe a sigh of relief that the really bad cuts hadn't happened.

Some of the suggestions in the documents were extremely radical and to the best of my knowledge have never been proposed anywhere else in the country either before or since. Proposals included banning non-urgent hospital treatment for anyone living outside of the Oxford region and imposing a time penalty on people moving in to the region before they could qualify for NHS treatment. Another idea proposed the wholesale scrapping of accident and emergency units, leaving just one in the county of Oxfordshire. And most controversially of all there were proposals to make NHS patients pay for non-urgent operations as well as getting rid of hospital catering and requiring families to bring in food when relatives were in hospital.

I suppose you could say the RHA was ahead of its time as far as the changing face of the NHS is concerned, but the *Oxford Mail* didn't see it that way. My story was splashed across the front page with a headline 'NHS under a new scalpel – cuts could save £12m a year'. This was accompanied by the heading 'Yet another *Oxford Mail* exclusive by Paul Dale', with a picture of me.

Over 40 years as a political reporter, many of my best stories, that is to say stories of maximum embarrassment to councils and health authorities, were only able to be written because elected politicians, and in a very few cases local authority officers, leaked confidential documents. The emergence of email with the ability to transfer council reports at the click of a button means that giving information to journalists is now just a few seconds work. But the determined leaker had better make sure he covers his tracks lest council IT bods uncover an embarrassing email trail.

I've often been asked what prompts public servants to feed journalists with sensitive information. There are complex answers to such a question. Sometimes, but not very often in my experience, the leaker believes that the public has an absolute right to know what elected representatives are up to and takes the view that nothing discussed at a council meeting should remain confidential. Others are largely driven by huge egos and leak information because they have been unwittingly sucked into what they regard as the glamorous world of journalism. They like to be seen drinking with newspaper reporters in pubs, they like to think they are important and influential people and with alcohol having loosened their tongues, these people are more likely to respond positively to that old journalistic trick of "let's have an off the record conversation".

Here's a tip for all politicians: there is no such thing as off the record. What a journalist hears cannot be unheard. It is the simplest thing in the world to keep an 'off the record' snippet to yourself for a few days and then, using the information you have been given, telephone other council members and MPs until someone is prepared to go on the record and confirm the story. You can then return to your informant and say 'some other people told me this, not you'. It really is very simple. Or find at least three people to confirm what you've been told, and publish: the best advice for politicians is if you know something that you really wouldn't want to see in a newspaper, a journalist is the last person you should tell.

The health brief led to my first major award as a reporter – Midland Journalist of the Year 1986 – for a series of exclusive reports about women in Oxford who sadly died from cervical cancer after smear tests were declared negative when they were in fact positive. Such circumstances would be equally tragic today, but 30 years ago the story created a sensation in an era when hospitals were generally regarded to be beacons of medical brilliance and human error was all too often brushed under the carpet. My coverage prompted a huge political reaction and resulted in a Statement to the House of Commons by Kenneth Clarke, then the Health Minister, who promised that such a thing should never happen again. The award, sponsored by the Heart of England Building Society, was presented at a ceremony held at the Birmingham Press Club and came with a cheque for £750 – a hefty amount in 1986, equivalent to almost a month's wages.

The award resulted indirectly in my departure from Oxford, when in September 1986 I became the *Coventry Evening Telegraph*'s political editor. My decision to move was reinforced by the new *Oxford Mail* editor Eddie Duller, who had taken over from Terry Page. The aptly named Duller called me into his office to 'congratulate' me on winning the prize and added rather dismissively that he wasn't really keen on reporters entering competitions and winning prizes because in his experience it meant you would leave soon and find another newspaper to work for.

Possibly, Duller simply had an odd sense of humour. But he was dead right about one thing because a week or so after he made his views known I spotted an advertisement in UK Press Gazette from the *Coventry Evening Telegraph* wishing to appoint a political editor. I applied and got the job, but I'd also applied to join BBC Radio Leicester as a general reporter. The BBC job interview left an indelible mark, but not for good reasons when it became clear that the interview board could not for a second even begin to comprehend why I had not gone to university. The reason, as I explained, was that my parents had very little money and I felt it right to find a job as soon as possible to support them financially. In these circumstances, a one-year journalism college course was preferable to a three-year university course. A woman on the interview panel who gave the impression of having a nasty smell under her nose shot me a withering glance: "But surely you could have got a grant to go to university?" I'd like to think a BBC interviewing panel would be more understanding today, but I'm not sure that would be the case.

In the year before my departure the *Oxford Mail* and *Times* began to plan for the introduction of new technology, with word processors replacing typewriters. But the management could not reach agreement with the National Union of Journalists about a wage rise to reflect the willingness of journalists to embrace change. A clandestine operation was set up by the editors to demonstrate the advantages of new technology to a few journalists who could be trusted to keep quiet. I was one of a handful selected to attend secret sessions at the newspaper's city centre office in New Inn Hall Street where some of the new machines were set up in a locked room on the first floor. We were fascinated by a glimpse into the future and the ease at which these amazing machines could be operated, so much more quickly than typewriters and with no further requirement for copy paper or the dreaded Tippex to correct mistakes.

Part IV

Coventry 1986-2000

Chapter Nineteen

Bacon Butties, Snooker and Golf

I n 1986 the *Coventry Evening Telegraph* remained under the ownership
of Lord Iliffe whose family founded the newspaper in 1891 and also
owned a stable of famous regional titles – the *Birmingham Post*, the
Birmingham Evening Mail, the *Sunday Mercury*, and the *Cambridge Evening
News*. The *Telegraph's* splendid Coventry city centre headquarters in
Corporation Street, built in 1957 with marble pillars and art deco touches,
were a stunning statement of Iliffe's wealth and represented one of the great
post-war regional newspaper buildings, a confident architectural statement
to herald the optimism of the late-1950s and worthy of a publication that in
its prime sold upwards of 130,000 copies a day.

Iliffe's newspapers took what was, even by the standards of the day, a
rather old-fashioned paternalistic approach to staff who were regarded as
being part of the '*Telegraph* family', and treated accordingly. The *Telegraph*
HQ boasted almost everything a person might need to improve the daily
working experience. It had a social club and a bar with table tennis and a
snooker room, as well as a subsidised staff canteen where hungry journalists,
printers and advertising staff queued to buy bacon and sausage rolls for
breakfast and could get a cheap two-course meal at lunchtime. You were
asked whether you wanted the bread roll dipped in a container of hot bacon
fat, and anyone wishing to show off and with no concern for their health could
request a 'double dip'. It wasn't unusual for reporters with time on their hands
to sneak off for an extended coffee break and a mid-morning frame of
snooker. I can't recall anyone at management level challenging such behaviour.

In the afternoon, ladies from the canteen trundled a tea trolley around
the entire building satisfying a never-ending need by the workforce for
doughnuts and sticky buns. Lardy cakes were a particular favourite on the
editorial floor. And for employees who perhaps felt a little queasy after
consuming too much cake, the company doctor called once a week to issue
prescriptions and even hand out sick notes, much to the annoyance of the
news desk.

The paper owned a sports ground in Lythalls Lane to the north of the city
where the *Evening Telegraph's* football and cricket teams had played for

years. The pavilion, which predictably enough featured a bar, was lined with photographs and cartoons of the company's sporting stars and it was notable that many present and past employees were related, giving an indication that for some Coventry households the *Telegraph* had been the family's employer for decades.

There was also the 21 Club, a tribute to those who had clocked up 21 years' unbroken service with the company. Once a year staff who had passed the long-service deadline would be given a day off work and were invited to a celebratory lunch. They'd be picked up free of charge in cars and taxis, taken to the beano, and then safely delivered home again. Upon reaching the 21-year milestone you'd be given a gift by the company such as a gold watch.

For editorial staff whose normal week was from Monday to Friday, weekend working was rewarded with a special wage supplement which I benefited from when visiting the party conferences – from memory, I believe it was £100 for Saturdays and £150 for Sundays. There was even a much-anticipated Christmas bonus linked to the company's profits, which usually worked out to be between one and two weeks' pay and certainly came in very useful at a time of the year when family finances are stretched. And as a specialist reporter, my quarterly home phone rental bill was paid by the company as well as a contribution towards the cost of calls.

The *Coventry Evening Telegraph Yearbook*, sold in local book shops, was published annually and listed biographical details of the great and good of Coventry and Warwickshire as well as council and general election results and details about the make-up of all local authorities in the paper's circulation area. Getting a mention marked you down as somebody of substance in the yearbook which was a sort of 'who's who' of the West Midlands.

New members of staff were required to report to the boardroom for a meeting with managing director F T 'Frank' Bunting where they would receive a fatherly chat about the career benefits that were likely to accrue now they were at the *CET*. Frank, who was born in 1930 near Leamington Spa, had devoted pretty much all of his working life to Iliffe newspapers and the *Evening Telegraph* and was a respected figure in the Coventry and Warwickshire business world.

A kindly man, although fully prepared to let you know he was the boss, my abiding memory of Frank shortly before he retired was standing next to him in Broadgate at a ceremony 1990 to remember the 50th anniversary of the Coventry blitz when more than 500 Luftwaffe bombers destroyed much of the city centre and killed an estimated 586 people. Vera Lynn, the 'Forces Sweetheart' was guest of honour at the gathering on a bitterly cold November night. Then in her early 70s and suitably insulated by an obviously extremely expensive fur coat, she rose without any musical accompaniment to sing pitch-perfect *(There'll be Bluebirds Over) The White Cliffs of Dover*. I glanced at Frank, who'd been a 10-year-old boy at the time of the blitz and had vivid memories of the death and destruction heaped on to Coventry. Tears were running uncontrollably down his face.

The managing director's office on the top floor of the *CET* building was part of the flat used by Lord Iliffe when he stayed in Coventry, which he did frequently, and much to the amusement of *CET* staff he would always be attended by his butler. In Lord Iliffe's absence, the flat's lounge area was the location for drinks receptions when the company wined and dined guests. It was evident that very little in terms of décor or furnishing had changed since the early 1960s even down to bottles of Double Diamond in the drinks' cabinet, said to be the favourite beer of Prince Philip. I always thought the room bore more than a passing resemblance to the shaky set from *Crossroads*, the Midland television soap opera.

A sumptuous wood-panelled boardroom doubled as a dining room and featured a large coffin-shaped table with a 'secret button' to trigger a bell hidden underneath, which Frank Bunting took an almost childish delight in surreptitiously pressing to alert kitchen staff that a course had been finished and plates needed to be cleared.

Once a year the *Telegraph* organised the Coventry and Warwickshire Design Awards to promote new-build and architectural excellence among restoration projects with local experts roped in to judge the entries under the chairmanship of an editorial executive. The judging panel would board a coach and spend a pleasant day visiting nominated buildings. The judges weren't paid for their time but were compensated with a free lunch, stopping off half way through the day at the *Telegraph* offices for glasses of sherry and to meet the editor while marvelling at the opulence of Lord Iliffe's flat. The paper ran a similar contest to find the Coventry and Warwickshire pub of the year, although competition among journalists to get on the pub judging panel was understandably somewhat more intense than that to join the design awards panel.

New recruits to the paper were encouraged to join the football and cricket clubs, make use of the social club, and most importantly of all from Frank's point of view, join the *Evening Telegraph* Golf Society. Frank was a keen golfer and the society was his pride and joy. Indeed, his opening gambit when introducing himself to me and other new starters was: "Does anyone here play golf?" I raised my hand to indicate that I did indeed play golf. Frank beamed fondly at me as if he'd discovered a long-lost son.

Regular matches were staged against leading Midland golf clubs and because the society was heavily subsidised by the company the cost of playing some good courses and eating a convivial dinner afterwards was very little indeed. My first decision on arriving at Coventry was to join the golf society which turned out to be rather like being in the soccer or rugby team at school. Members were permitted to finish work in the middle of the afternoon so they could represent the company at golf, much to the fury of news editors who were powerless to protest because they could hardly question the wishes of the managing director.

Frank was not above a little gamesmanship on the golf course. We were playing for the annual society championship at Stratford-upon-Avon Golf Club and I was in the lead with Frank a close second. As I attempted to tee off and took my club back there came from behind me the unmistakable sound of water sprinkling. The managing director was noisily spending a penny in the nearest bush.

Although Frank always claimed never to interfere in editorial decisions, he did not hold back from making his views known and once sought me out to ask why a leading article I had written for the paper featured the word 'spin doctor'. What is a spin doctor, Frank wanted to know? He was unimpressed with American slang creeping into the *Coventry Evening Telegraph*.

Chapter Twenty

The Editor

Geoffrey Elliott was the editor of the *Coventry Evening Telegraph* in 1986. It's fair to say that Geoff was a Marmite man in many respects – your either liked him, or disliked him. There weren't many people who had neutral opinions about Geoff Elliott. I admired his professionalism, his sound news values, his enthusiasm for politics, his conviction, putting it mildly, that Coventry council was not a very well-run local authority, his insistence on good grammar, and most of all his refusal to put up with shirkers and a failure to suffer fools gladly, which obviously put him on a collision course with a few of those he had to work with. He fought to encourage newspaper owners to reward journalists with decent wages, campaigned successfully against the Thatcher government's proposal to introduce identity cards, and was one of the first regional editors to use his newspaper to put the case for reform of the archaic Sunday trading laws.

The *Telegraph* published four Coventry editions in 1986 beginning with a Lunch edition with a deadline of about 10am for all copy to be away from the news room followed by a Late City edition published at 2pm, a City Final edition, for which all copy had to be away from the newsroom by about 2.30pm, and a Night Final which was sold at factory gates as workers were leaving for home at 5.30pm. There were also separate Warwickshire editions produced by district offices covering Nuneaton and Bedworth, Rugby, Warwick and Leamington and Stratford-upon-Avon.

This meant it was possible for a breaking news story to be with the subs as late as 5pm for the Night Final, giving *Telegraph* readers the certainty that the product they were buying on their way home was as up to date as possible. The Night Final carried the day's horse racing results which made it a must-buy for keen followers of the turf.

The popularity of the *Evening Telegraph* was such that, even by 1986 when circulation had already peaked, between 70 and 80 percent of homes in some parts of the city had the paper delivered and in a few streets the penetration figure was as high as 90 percent.

In common with many other evening newspapers at the time, the *Evening Telegraph* published a separate sports edition on Saturday evenings. The 'Pink', so called because it was printed on pink paper, carried all the results from that day's sporting events, national and local football, rugby and cricket, as well as weekly round-ups for darts, cribbage and dominoes in pub leagues and was a must-read in the homes, pubs and clubs of the city from 1946 to 2004, when it ceased publication having been put out of business partly by the ready availability of sporting information on satellite television and via the internet but also by the growing trend of Premier League football matches switching kick offs from Saturdays to Sundays and playing more games in mid-week.

Soon after my arrival at the *Evening Telegraph*, a monumental event occurred in the city's sporting history. Unfashionable Coventry City FC won the FA cup for the first and only time in the club's history, beating favourites Tottenham Hotspur 3-2 at Wembley. The unexpected victory delivered a massive, albeit short-lived, confidence boost to the city. Overnight, Coventry became a joyous sea of sky-blue shirts and flags and the victory triggered a drunken party that seemed to go on for several weeks. Work colleagues who hitherto had shown little or no interest in Coventry City professed to be lifelong fans, although one young reporter made something of a fool of himself by attending a match at the club's Highfield Road ground and attempting to pay at the turnstiles with an American Express card. Even the city council stepped up to the mark by organising an open-bus tour for the winning side followed by a civic reception. The bus that carried the players is now on display at Coventry Transport Museum.

Geoff Elliott was a hands-on editor in a manner I had not experienced before or since and took the trouble to scrutinise each edition of the *Evening Telegraph* to select what he liked and what he did not like. A steady stream of pithy hand-written notes to reporters and news editors would emerge during the week from the editor's office delivered by Geoff's secretary, and on a Friday a week's round-up by the editor would be pinned on the noticeboard – dubbed the 'sheet of shame' by reporters. Sometimes these would praise a good story, but more often than not would contain blunt, very public, criticism of poor grammar, slang, missing hyphens, spelling mistakes, unnecessary puns, and worst of all getting someone's name wrong.

One of the first things pointed out to me by the news desk upon arriving at the *Telegraph* was the existence of a list of words banned from the paper including 'local' as in 'a local man' and 'situation', both words having been deemed meaningless by the editor. A former colleague recalls when, as a raw trainee in 1987 having written a front-page story about drunken men fighting in the streets, she was ordered by a news editor to spin the piece up by writing "drink-fuelled yobs" into the opening paragraph, which she duly did. The editor took exception to this, chastised the reporter, and used his Friday sheet of shame to ban the phrase "drink-fuelled yobs". The news editor concerned did at least have the decency to apologise to the reporter, but probably not to the editor.

The only occasion 'situation' or 'local' could appear was in a direct quote. So great was Geoff Elliott's influence over me that it has only been in recent years that I've dared to use 'local' or 'situation' when writing, and even now I half expect a snotty note to be winging its way to my desk.

Geoff attempted to keep a firm grip on the editorial department. One of his first questions at my job interview was to ask whether I was now or had ever been a member of a political party. I could truthfully answer that I was not, had not and did not intend to be. He took the view his political editor should not be a member of a political party, expressed a wish that all editorial staff should live in Coventry or Warwickshire, and on the day of the 1987 General Election Labour-supporting reporters were barred from wearing red roses in their buttonholes, an entirely correct decision for a politically neutral newspaper in my view.

It seemed a given to me that the political editor and the editor of a local regional newspaper would steer clear of joining a political party, for to do so would obviously result in claims of bias if the affiliation became widely known. It wasn't until later in my career in newspapers that I discovered two of my editors were lifelong card-carrying members of the Labour party. One let details of his membership slip out casually while we were chatting. He had to rush home to do some canvassing, adding that for obvious reasons he didn't get involved publicly, but he had 'certain obligations' to work for the party. This was said in a matter of fact way as if it was entirely reasonable and commonplace for a newspaper editor to play an active role in a political party. Call me naïve, but I'd simply assumed that newspapers taking a non-party political stance would have editors of a similarly independent viewpoint. Or at the very least, if an editor did lean one way, as did Tony Price with his obvious support for the Thatcher governments, he'd make sure his political editor was in the picture.

I felt obliged to tell Geoff at my interview that I was no longer a member of the National Union of Journalists. I'd resigned while at Oxford where the NUJ had fallen under the control of Trotskyists and the hard-left and seemed to me to exist solely to stir up trouble with the management. This represented a big change in my working career. I'd been an active NUJ member at Reading, becoming deputy Father of the Chapel (vice-chair of the office branch), and fully supported a six-week strike for improved pay and conditions in the late 1970s. We had no strike pay from the NUJ, typically, so to make some money while off work I turned my hand to labouring for a local house-building chum. And, yes, it was a bit too much like hard work compared with the cushy life of a journalist.

At Oxford, after one particularly pointless strike, I resigned as a union member, much to the astonishment of colleagues, pretty much all of whom were on the left and committed NUJ members. Newspaper editorial floors at that time were dominated by the NUJ. It was extremely rare for a journalist below management level not to be a member and almost impossible for a non-union member to make it to Fleet Street. I explained to Geoff the circumstances behind my decision, and he said he wasn't at all concerned. Some of my new colleagues thought differently, though, and made it clear they thought I ought to 'show solidarity' by re-joining. I declined.

One of Geoff Elliott's initial tasks on taking the editor's chair in 1980 was to appoint a political editor, the first time the paper had bothered with such a role. He wanted the *Coventry Evening Telegraph* to join the first division of regional newspapers along with the likes of the *Birmingham Post*, the *Yorkshire Post* and the *Glasgow Herald*, and that meant having a political editor based in Coventry as well as someone in Westminster with a Commons lobby pass who could provide a national political service for the paper's readers.

One of the things that made the *Evening Telegraph* stand out was a fearless ability to comment on current events through a leader column of about 800 words running down the length of the letters page in which the *Telegraph* had its say on issues of the day, both local and national. The column won national awards for Geoff, but he didn't have the time to write every leader and therefore needed a team of writers to help him. I quickly became one of three or four leader writers and attended the leader conference held directly after the main editorial conference first thing in the morning.

With Geoff in the chair alongside features editor Chris Arnot, features writer Peter Walters, and deputy editor Roger Monkman, we'd discuss possible subjects worthy of *Evening Telegraph* comment and writing duties would be allocated. The leader writers never openly discussed their own personal politics, although it was fairly obvious Arnot and Walters were firmly on the left, while Monkman and I occupied the centre ground. Geoff Elliott's politics remained a closely guarded secret. There were claims he supported the new SDP, but this was never substantiated.

I'd write my 200-300 words, generally criticising the city council or the government, and wait nervously for the editor's comments, which were sometimes supportive, but quite often critical of dodgy grammar and the use of superfluous words. Many of my colleagues hated being the victim of criticism from the editor, but I found it constructive and believe it made me a far better writer.

The paper's stance on matters involving sex could be prudish, to say the least. In 1984, two years before I arrived, a display at the Herbert Art Gallery by Coventry lecturer John Yeadon featuring 'torture and sexual abuse' prompted a thunderous *CET* leader article, condemning the pictures as "the product of a contorted mind sated by self-gratification and an immature desire to shock and repel". The leader writer, by now worked up into a state of considerable anger, concluded: "These pictures, as any schoolboy would tell them, unpleasantly represent various homosexual acts." Sadly, the passing of time did nothing to soften these occasional puritanical tendencies. In 1999 the James Bond spoof film 'Austin Powers: The Spy Who Shagged Me' was released much to the fury of the dear old *CET*, which railed in a leader (not written by me) against the lowering of standards and unnecessary use of foul language in a film likely to be seen by young people.

It would be an understatement to say that Geoff Elliott and Coventry Council did not generally see eye to eye. Elliott joined the paper after attending Bablake school in Coventry, which was founded in 1344 and is one of the oldest independent schools in the country. This did not endear him to certain Labour councillors who regarded anything that came out of 'elitist' Bablake with the utmost suspicion. Elliott had been a star writer on the *Telegraph* and after moving into the editor's chair he introduced a no-holds-barred gossip column which, in a nod to the Lady Godiva legend, was called *Peeping Tom*. Published weekly, *Peeping Tom* was full of articles designed to prick the egos and pomposity of Coventry and Warwickshire councillors, MPs, and other public figures. Reporters were encouraged to provide snippets for *Peeping Tom*, and since they were rewarded with £5 for each piece that was used there was never any shortage of juicy copy from my pen.

The deputy news editor was Geoff Grimmer. A New Zealander who came to Britain in the 1950s, he claimed to have arrived in London as a young man with nothing but a cardboard suitcase containing his worldly possessions. Grimmer had worked his way up from a tough background and was a stickler for accuracy in the newspaper.

He also suffered from a recurring nightmare common to all news editors that he would arrive at work and discover there were no stories for the next day's paper. With this in mind, he kept a store of articles in reserve hidden in his desk – Geoff Grimmer's bottom drawer, as it became known. The problem with this strategy was that decent stories were sometimes held back for days, or even weeks, which was a frustrating experience for reporters.

Grimmer was worried about what would happen to his drawer full of stories when reporters switched from typewriters to word processors. He was assured that an electronic 'basket' would be incorporated into the new system for overnight stories, which as far as Grimmer was concerned meant a stash of stories for several days to come.

The task of monitoring news programmes on Coventry's independent radio station *Mercia Sound* to check whether the *Evening Telegraph* had missed anything also fell to Geoff Grimmer who would regularly dash over to the politics desk flapping his arms and declaring that *Mercia* were running a fantastic city council story and why hadn't we got it? Investigation showed that more often than not the story in question had been in the *Telegraph* several days or even weeks previously.

A rivalry, usually friendly, existed between Geoff Elliott and *Mercia Sound* MD Stuart Linnell and Geoff took it to heart if the radio station beat his newspaper to a story particularly since *Mercia* employed only a handful of journalists compared to the *Evening Telegraph*'s 50-plus workforce.

The notion that commercial radio stations could ever provide a news service comprehensive enough to persuade listeners to stop buying papers always seemed nonsensical to me, but it was the case that most regional newspapers in the mid-1980s were increasingly jumpy over what they regarded as dangerous competition on their doorstep.

Geoff Grimmer regarded female reporters with some suspicion in as far as what he would have regarded as 'men's jobs' were concerned. One day he had to find someone to go out and interview a man who had built his own motorbike. Gazing desperately around the newsroom to find a suitable petrol-head male to whom the task could be allotted, Grimmer could see only one reporter – a young woman. "But she'll never know what questions to ask," he complained loudly to anyone in listening distance. Luckily, the resourceful woman turned in a story good enough to satisfy even Grimmer.

The *Coventry Telegraph* news editor in 1986, Alan Kirby, hailed from Rugby and joined the paper after leaving school, working his way up through the ranks to gain the nickname 'Scoop' by providing a relentless stream of mainly crime-based stories. Upon hearing a police, fire or ambulance siren wailing through the city centre, the ever-enthusiastic Kirby would leap to his feet and imitating the siren scream "nee, naa, nee, naa", yelling at the nearest reporter to find out what was going on and "get out there".

My interview for the Coventry job was the longest I ever encountered, lasting about two hours in total, which must have been worrying for my wife who was waiting anxiously in a nearby car park. I think I told her I'd be about half an hour. The first part consisted of being quizzed by deputy editor Roger Monkman and news editor Alan Kirby, neither of whom appeared to have much knowledge of or interest in politics. They asked who I thought would win the next election. I said Mrs Thatcher would enjoy a clear victory which was my firm belief, but a bit of gamble to admit it given the left-wing instincts of most journalists and the disastrous impact of the prime minister's economic policies on the West Midlands' industrial base. As it turned out, both of my interviewers gave the distinct impression that they would not think it a disaster if Maggie stormed to another victory, as indeed she did.

They had heard about something called a community charge that would replace the household rates system if Margaret Thatcher won the next General Election. What was my view on this? As luck would have it I did know about the community charge having recently written about the subject in depth for the *Oxford Times*, so I was able to give a detailed account of how every adult in the country would have to make a financial contribution under the new system however poor they might be and how this would almost certainly prove to be highly controversial.

Monkman and Kirby disappeared into the editor's office and I could clearly hear shouts of: "Geoff, Geoff, this bloke knows all about the bloody community charge for Christ's sake."

I was sure the job was mine at that stage, but I still had to face a lengthy grilling by Geoff Elliott.

Staffing arrangements at the *Coventry Evening Telegraph* in 1986 would make today's journalists green with envy at the vast number of people employed. A list of staff telephone numbers issued to employees, which I still have today, shows that there were 21 reporters based at the head office as well as a business editor, a political editor, four on the news desk, a picture editor and deputy picture editor, and seven photographers. There were district offices at Nuneaton, Bedworth, Leamington, Rugby and Stratford. The Nuneaton office had three reporters and one photographer, Leamington had three reporters and one photographer, Rugby had two reporters and one photographer, Stratford and Bedworth had one reporter each.

The *CET* library was staffed by four full-timers. There were secretaries for the editor, news desk, sports editor and features editor as well as the managing director. In fact, there were so many secretaries over different parts of the building that the editor and deputy editor hosted an annual Christmas lunch party for them.

The paper boasted a 59-strong editorial department excluding copy boys and girls, young men and women whose job was to listen for shouts of 'copy' from the subs and collect finished stories and place them in tubes that would then be whizzed downstairs through a pneumatic suction system to the composing room where they would be typeset ready for printing.

But 1986 was by no means the high-water mark for the editorial department. By 1999 staffing levels were even more generous with 25 reporters and news desk staff, 10 sports writers and subs, 17 sub-editors, six feature writers, ten district office reporters and photographers, five librarians, six other staff attached to the library, an editor and deputy editor, and two secretaries, making a grand total of 83 employees.

Chapter Twenty-One

The Town Wall

There was a considerable daytime drinking culture at the *Telegraph*, but only among those who were senior enough or bold enough to escape from the control of news editors who had their work cut out attempting to make sure lunch breaks did not extend beyond an hour. My seniority meant that I was not subject to such restrictions, thankfully, and could leave the office as and when I wished.

The office pub was the Town Wall Tavern, a boozer of Georgian origins about 200 yards from the *Telegraph* building next to the Belgrade Theatre. This ancient hostelry, which is still very much part of the Coventry pub scene, has been extended over the years but still features what is claimed to be the smallest bar in the country with its own serving counter, a tiny room at the front of the building nicknamed the Donkey Box capable of accommodating no more than about a half a dozen people in comfort.

The Donkey Box was the venue for hard-drinking Christmas lunches held by the *Evening Telegraph* sports desk with a dining table and chairs shoehorned into the room and fancy dress the order of the day. In fact, the *Telegraph*'s sports writers were very keen supporters of the Town Wall Tavern as well as the nearby Gatehouse pub and several other city centre hostelries and were known for early doors trips to the pub at about 11.00 after the first edition of the day had been printed, and would revisit at regular intervals thereafter until going home time. Sports staff were in the habit of leaving jackets on the backs of their chairs to give the impression that they were somewhere in the building rather than at the pub or the bookies, but the cunning plan didn't end so well on one occasion when a sudden downpour left the intrepid drinkers soaking wet on returning to the office.

When word processors and computers were introduced at the *Telegraph* the sports editor and his drinking companion sports sub, in a fine example of newspaper humour, made a point of selecting as their passwords 'Mitchell' and 'Butler' in a nod to Mitchells & Butlers, the West Midlands brewery that in those days owned the Town Wall Tavern and scores of other Coventry and Warwickshire pubs. The ability to drink copious amounts of alcohol and still produce a newspaper was something that the sports desk was very proud of.

As former *Evening Telegraph* football and rugby writer Steve Evans wrote on Facebook: "We invented the staggered lunch break. We walked to the pub, and staggered back."

The Town Wall was crammed five days a week between the hours of 12 noon and 2.30pm with *Telegraph* editorial staff. Features Editor Chris Arnot held court there alongside deputy editor Roger Monkman, sports editor Roger Draper, and George Booth, chairman of the Coventry licensing magistrates, as well as the fiercely eccentric intellectual Rob Gill, the proprietor of what is now Coventry's only second-hand bookshop, Gosford Books. The pub was also a haunt for employees from the nearby British Gas and Equity and Law headquarters in the days when business types indulged in lengthy alcoholic lunches. Coventry's earthy wit and wisdom was available in spades at the Town Wall Tavern, where an anecdote which is most likely apocryphal but I'd like to think was true had it that a German tourist came into the bar and asked for directions to Coventry Cathedral, to be told: "You 'ad no trouble finding the fucker in 1940."

Booth, who hailed from Yorkshire but lived in Coventry for most of his life, owned a hostel for homeless people which he had inherited from his father. George was a man with strong opinions about what he saw as the demise of his adoptive city which he would broadcast across the pub after a few pints of Bass. Week after week he was routinely aghast to discover, yet again, his comments plastered all over the *Telegraph* in the shape of *Peeping Tom* and would demand to know who on earth could have leaked such information to a newspaper. No one dared to say: "George, it was you".

Once a year Booth would preside over what were known as the Brewster Sessions – annual meetings of licensing justices to deal with the grant, renewal, and transfer of licences to sell intoxicating liquor. This gave him an opportunity to expand on familiar themes, drunkenness among young people and badly run pubs, neither of which he assured the great Coventry public would be tolerated on his watch.

Booth, oddly enough the holder of a black belt in the martial art Taekwondo, was predictably labelled 'General George Booth' by *Peeping Tom*. He was friendly with senior Coventry police officer Superintendent Bill Guest, whose Town Wall promises to clear up crime in the city earned him the nickname 'Two-Gun Billy'. Geoffrey Dear, who took over as West Midlands chief constable in 1985, was unamused at the irreverent way the *Evening Telegraph* treated his force, often depicted as incompetent gun-toting cowboys by *Peeping Tom*. Dear complained about the coverage, but the chief constable's intervention, I am happy to say, seemed to have no impact on *Peeping Tom*'s determination week after week to stick two fingers up to those in authority.

Booth's career as a JP ended sadly when he was convicted of drink-driving and was obliged to resign as chairman of the licensing magistrates. Some of Booth's friends at the *CET* were horrified when the paper put his picture on the front page accompanied by a story revealing he had been charged with driving while under the influence. They'd thought, wrongly, that his close association with the *Coventry Telegraph* would have been sufficient to give him a measure of protection from public humiliation and that the story, if it had to be used at all, would be hidden away towards the back of the paper. Booth always claimed he was not over the limit and had been 'set up' by establishment figures who found him too outspoken. Whatever the truth of this, not for the first time, an establishment figure discovered far too late that there is no such thing as a friendly newspaper when seeking protection from a scandal. George Booth died in 2018, aged 81.

Geoff Elliott wisely steered clear of the Town Wall, but on one memorable occasion he and a guest appeared in the main bar at the height of the lunch time crush. I'd never seen a pub empty so quickly, with sports subs in particular falling over each other to get into the lounge bar and out of a side door to avoid the editor's steely gaze.

The Donkey Box was also the venue for 'alternative leaving presentations' for journalists departing from the company after having fallen out with management and who were as a result penalised by being denied a traditional leaving speech and presentation on the editorial floor. These occasions usually involved reporters who had been lured to better paid jobs in London while still trainees, a development viewed with horror by the traditionalist *Coventry Telegraph* news desk. I recall having to deliver at least two Donkey Box leaving speeches for political reporters as I was determined they should leave with good wishes from their colleagues even though they were being denied a formal leaving presentation thanks to the petty attitude of *CET* management.

The *Evening Telegraph*'s annual Christmas lunch was an occasion not to be missed as upwards of 150 representatives of Coventry and Warwickshire's political, business and sporting elite crammed into Lord Iliffe's reception rooms to enjoy a sumptuous buffet and unlimited drink. Council leaders would mingle with chief constables and MPs, and the wine would flow liberally. But the event inevitably caused some friction among the more junior editorial staff since only senior and specialist reporters were supposed to attend and in order to book their place had to provide a list of guests they wanted to invite to the bash.

The news desk feared, with some justification, that the entire reporting staff and sub editors would sneak off to the lunch and not be seen again that day, leaving a chronic shortage of stories for the next day's paper. You'd be asked what time your guests would be arriving, between the starting time of 12 and finishing time of 3.30. This, presumably, was to prevent reporters hogging the entire three and a half hours. It didn't work, obviously. I'd simply say some of my guests were arriving early, some half way through and some towards the end.

Consequently, the editor's secretary and the news desk secretary stood guard at the entrance to the party with a list of invited journalists in their hands to make sure the more junior members of staff did not sneak in. The Christmas bash, which must have cost a small fortune to put on, was one of many *CET* traditions to disappear in the late 1990s as editorial budget cuts began to bite.

In 1987 I organised the first Christmas dinner for my political desk colleagues, something that became an *Evening Telegraph* institution for the next ten years. We'd generally invite a few guests and kick off proceedings with champagne at the Town Wall before moving on to a decent eating place with a favourite spot being the Pagoda Chinese restaurant which, bizarrely, was positioned on the second floor of one of the city centre's blocks of council flats. Despite its odd location the Pagoda was for many years the best Chinese restaurant in Coventry and also gave pride of place to one of the columns I wrote as the *Telegraph*'s restaurant critic – headline: "Pagoda is a towering success."

The newspapers were printed on the *CET*'s Corporation Street site and distributed across the West Midlands by a fleet of vans, instantly recognisable by the *Evening Telegraph* livery, which were a common sight on the roads of Coventry and Warwickshire.

By the 2000s, the savings that could be achieved by scrapping in-house delivery teams became a key consideration for many newspapers like the *CET* that decided to cease to be evening papers and switch to morning publication. By doing this they were able to 'piggy back' onto national newspaper delivery operations, thereby getting rid of fleets of expensive vans and sacking delivery drivers. The downside, of course, was that *CET* readers were not being served with the most up to date news when their one-edition morning newspaper arrived on the doorstep.

In 2006 the *CET* began printing the next day's paper the previous night and distributing it the following morning, with the result that customers were in danger of reading distinctly old news by the time they bought the paper.

The *Coventry Telegraph's* owners, Trinity Mirror, now called Reach, argued that anyone could access up to the minute news via the paper's website, which is undoubtedly the case, although whether some of what is available counts as news is a matter for debate. What is undeniable is that the *Coventry Telegraph* circulation was a paltry 7,218 a day in 2020 according to the Audit Bureau of Circulation, a far cry from the days when, as an evening newspaper, circulation stood at 85,000 in 1994 and over 100,000 in the early 1980s.

Chapter Twenty-Two

The Way We Were

The large number of editorial employees at the *CET* in 1986 pretty much guaranteed sufficient output to fill the newspapers and meant that anyone with a disinclination to work was able to get away with doing very little indeed. One colleague, I quickly noticed, routinely arrived at about 9.30, blaming heavy traffic for holding him up, proceeded to read the national newspapers for half an hour or so, wandered aimlessly around the newsroom chatting to colleagues, and then generally disappeared to the canteen for a bacon and egg roll.

One reporter operated an unethical and unofficial system with regard to a number of Labour city councillors who he favoured. He freely admitted to having a 'protected list' of councillors who, in return for feeding him sensitive information, would be saved from bad publicity. Those not on the protected list – the majority of councillors – would be hung out to dry. I made it my business as political editor to make sure that the protected councillors were protected no longer.

One or two reporters strolled in at about 9.15 in the morning and were gone by 4.30. But the majority put in far more hours than they were contracted to work for because they enjoyed the job and believed they were producing a first-class product. During my time in Coventry I generally started work at 7.30am and did not usually finish until pub opening time after 5pm, although that was entirely my choice. In fact, I cannot recall ever being given starting and finishing times. It was simply a case in those halcyon days before HR existed of turn up, write as many stories as you can, and go home.

Formal assessments of individual performance and personal development plans did not exist for journalists on most regional newspapers until the mid-1990s when managements and HR departments began to insist on systems of measuring output and ability. Any such attempts at regulation were always opposed by reporters, and even by some editors, with claims that a journalist could not possibly be compared with, say, someone manufacturing widgets in a factory and it would be misleading to delve too deeply into performance, which was simply a convenient argument for those people whose shortcomings were at risk of being exposed by such assessments.

By the 2000s, as the *Coventry Evening Telegraph*'s circulation and advertising fell and new owners came along and insisted on ever higher profits, the editorial department would be pruned significantly. When reporters and photographers left, they were not always replaced, district editions of the paper were scaled back or scrapped and district offices were closed. Unsurprisingly, given the scale of diminishing local content, newspaper sales continued to fall.

The internet opened up access to information 24 hours a day and people found they no longer needed to buy a local newspaper to get the football results or to look at advertising for property and cars – everything you wanted was simply there, mostly for free, at the click of a button.

By 2010 the appearance of smart phones capable of sending a story via email and taking pictures of a good enough quality to be published led to the rise of the so-called citizen reporter and some newspaper owners convinced themselves they could publish a good enough product with almost no journalists at all. The pace of change was so swift that only 15 years before in the mid-1990s the *Evening Telegraph*'s picture editor had been resisting the move towards using digital photography in the paper and insisted on keeping his dark room. Whether people have stopped buying newspapers because they are getting their news from elsewhere, or whether they are simply fed up with the lack of substance in today's newspapers is a conundrum that will probably never be answered satisfactorily.

Chapter Twenty-Three

Changing Coventry and the Poll Tax

When I arrived in 1986 Coventry was a city in transition. Tens of thousands of manufacturing jobs had been lost since 1979 and were yet to be replaced by anything substantial. The few remaining coal mines of north Warwickshire were closing, condemning families in the former pit villages to unemployment and an uncertain future. Plans to open a new pit to the south-west of Coventry, the so-called Superpit, which would have created and safeguarded hundreds of jobs, prompting thousands of words of comment in the *Evening Telegraph* over three years, were eventually dropped after British Coal deemed the project unprofitable.

At the height of the early 1980s recession 20,000 jobs disappeared in Coventry in a single week, a staggering statistic underlining the impact that the Tory Government's economic policy was having on the country's manufacturing heartlands.

Industrial wipe-out on such a scale came as a shock to me, cossetted as I had been living in relatively affluent Oxfordshire. I had read, of course, about the unemployment crisis, but witnessing the social cost face to face was quite another matter. Looking back now at this period of history it seems to me that the Thatcher governments were right to put paid to clearly unprofitable industries, but made a terrible mistake by failing to draw up adequate plans to replace the closed pits and factories with fresh employment. The notion that the market would simply step in and create new jobs turned out to be wildly optimistic, and it should have been obvious that such a transition was unlikely to happen quickly enough to come to the rescue of an entire generation who were exposed to mass unemployment and hardship.

Another area I found myself woefully uninformed about was the ethnic mix of the West Midlands, in particular the Muslim community which was beginning to make considerable inroads into the Labour party. I had no idea when I arrived in Coventry of what the Muslim faith stood for and managed to embarrass myself at lunch by handing a wine list to someone who I later discovered was a strict Muslim and forbidden to drink alcohol.

It was the sharp contrast between the good days and the bad days that made Coventry's plight stand out above many other Midland cities. In the 1970s the automotive industry was so vibrant with wages about 25 per cent higher than in other parts of the country that it was claimed a Coventry car worker could be sacked in the morning and secure new employment in a different factory by the end of the afternoon. Two decades later, Coventry's manufacturing sector was in disarray and even world-famous firms like tool makers Alfred Herbert went out of business because they could not compete with cheaper foreign imports. Unemployment was soaring, violent crime was on the increase. The city centre, flattened by Hitler's bombers during the war, rebuilt in the 1950s, and pedestrianised in the 1970s, was looking increasingly tired and in need of a radical makeover.

In 1981, Coventry 2 Tone band The Specials released *Ghost Town*, which went on to spend three weeks at number one in the charts. The third verse seemed to sum up the anger and disillusionment of young people:

> *This town (town) is coming like a ghost town*
> *Why must the youth fight against themselves?*
> *Government leaving the youth on the shelf*
> *This place (town) is coming like a ghost town*
> *No job to be found in this country*
> *Can't go on no more*
> *The people getting angry*

Coventry City Council had been under Labour control since 1979 and the party would remain in charge until 2003. Only the briefest of Conservative interludes ever crops up in Coventry – the Tories generally manage to win control at times when the Labour party nationally is particularly unpopular – from 1978 to 1979 and from 2006 to 2008. As for the Liberals and latterly the Liberal Democrats, the party has rarely made any inroads at all in Coventry, leaving the council in a permanent two-party state between mostly Labour and occasionally Conservative rule.

In 1986 the council was run by a Labour establishment consisting largely of unimaginative middle-aged men, many originally from Scotland, Wales, and Ireland, whose families had migrated to Coventry to find jobs in the city's factories after the Second World War. They'd climbed the trade union ladder to become shop stewards or union officials, and some, regardless of ability, were rewarded with jobs for life by being selected to stand for the council in many of the safest Labour wards in the country. Pretty much every Labour councillor, with only a few exceptions, regarded the media with thinly disguised contempt and managed to convince themselves that journalists accurately reporting the council's shortcomings were little more than Tory agents. Such was the atmosphere of suspicion that I recall coming under attack for wearing a blue tie to a council meeting, something that convinced the more hysterical Labour councillors that I was demonstrating support for the Conservative party. After much searching through the men's clothing shops of Coventry, I bought a 'council' tie with a red and blue pattern which I felt would suitably confuse my critics.

The council appeared to be trapped in the past with little or no interest in doing things differently or attempting to embrace partnership working with the private sector. As if to underline this approach, monthly full council meetings began with the ludicrous sight of the Lord Mayor emerging from the parlour accompanied by clerks bedecked in 19th century wigs, gowns and swords, an absurd imitation of the Speaker of the House of Commons. This bizarre parade continued into the 1990s and was briefly brought to a halt when the council's new chief executive, Iain Roxburgh, suffered with a fit of the giggles at having to dress up in such a way.

Rather than sitting in a press gallery, media representatives covering Coventry council meetings were required to occupy a table underneath the Lord Mayor's podium, staring straight into the faces of often hostile city councillors a few feet away. It was like being in a goldfish bowl, and intimidating to say the least. Oddly, Birmingham city council has the same media arrangements. It must be a West Midlands thing.

Coventry was a rather grim place in the mid-1980s, knocked about by economic recession, and with a council that all too often appeared to know the cost of everything and the value of nothing. The *Evening Telegraph* occasionally challenged the city council to do something to commemorate Coventry's claim to fame as the birthplace of the poet Philip Larkin, name a road after him or commission a statue for instance. But nothing was ever done. As far as the council was concerned, Larkin may as well have never existed. There were various theories about this, the most newsworthy being that Larkin's father, Sydney Larkin, Coventry city council Treasurer before the Second World War, was alleged to have been a Nazi sympathiser who attended two Nuremburg rallies during the 1930s and was said to have been so keen on Germany that he strutted around his house in lederhosen.

While it would be amusing to imagine that there was an ancient civic feud against the 'Nazi Larkins', my view is that the council as it existed in 1986 simply didn't have the leadership with a broad enough interest in the arts to concern itself with celebrating a poet. All of the political capital was aimed at running public services during a period of diminishing financial resources and attempting to keep the manufacturing sector afloat, with little success. Whether the council embraces Philip Larkin as part of Coventry City of Culture 2021 remains to be seen. Sadly, the evidence that has emerged in recent years showing Larkin to have been a keen fan of pornography and a closet racist suggests his time may have come and gone. Read his poems by all means, but perhaps we should leave Larkin the man on the shelf.

In 1986, all of the Coventry Labour councillors were white, most were men who hailed from the centre-right of the party and were allied closely to the more moderate trade unions. Although Coventry has had a significant Asian population since the early 1960s, it wasn't until 1987 that Labour managed to select a non-white face in a winnable ward, with Raj Malhotra picking up a seat in Lower Stoke. Even then, rather than giving themselves a pat on the back for finally overcoming what had clearly been an unofficial colour bar, Coventry's Labour establishment regarded Malhotra with suspicion because he was suspected of supporting the hard-left of the party.

The 1980s saw the rise of Militant, a hard-left pressure group within Labour which in common with Momentum today fought to restore 'real socialist policies' to the party's election manifesto. Militant supporters were mostly, but not exclusively, young people whose mobility meant they could move in to rented houses in wards and constituencies represented by moderate Labour councillors and use their combined voting power to force through the deselection of right-wing Labour councillors. This was not as difficult a task at it may seem since ward and constituency Labour party meetings were thinly attended at the best of times, so the unexpected arrival of a dozen or so new members who were Militant supporters could easily provide enough voting power to deselect centre-right councillors.

The Militant campaign in Coventry South-east, however, concentrated not simply on enthusing disaffected young people, but targeting long-term local residents, often middle-aged or older, who had become disillusioned with the local Labour party. In 1979, when Dave Nellist became chair of the Coventry South-east CLP, six out of the constituency's 12 councillors were Labour. By the late 1980s all 12 councillors were Labour.

The Trotskyist tactic of entryism shook the Labour Party to its core, not just in Coventry but in cities across the country. After all, if hard-left activists could mobilise so efficiently, no one on the centre-right of the party could consider themselves to be entirely safe from deselection including the Labour leader of Coventry City Council, Peter Lister, who was deselected but managed to confound his critics by finding and winning another seat.

Dave Nellist, one of the best-known Militant supporters in the country, sounded warning bells to Labour in 1983 when he was chosen to be the candidate in Coventry South-east, replacing the moderate Labour MP Bill Wilson who was standing down. Nellist ran as "a worker's MP on a worker's wage" and vowed to take only the wage of a skilled factory worker and donate the rest of an MP's salary to the Labour movement and charitable causes – a principle he followed throughout his parliamentary career. He was eventually expelled from the Labour Party for being a member of Militant in 1992.

In 1989 Militant reaped the benefit of an incredible own goal by the Tory government when the community charge, or poll tax as it became known, replaced household rates. Council tenants did not until then pay rates separately. Their portion of rates was amalgamated into weekly rental charges, with those on benefits ending up paying very little. The lowest earners paid nothing at all toward rent or rates. By contrast, under the government's initial plan, every adult had to pay the community charge in full, regardless of individual income.

As a result of the changes, low-paid and unemployed people from working class communities were suddenly faced for the first time with finding substantial sums of money to meet the demands of councils like Coventry, with total bills of £1,000 for a husband and wife not uncommon. Nicholas Ridley, the Tory Environment Secretary, insisted the new flat-rate system was fair by pointing out that "a Duke will pay the same as a dustman". It was, to put it mildly, an unfortunate and inflammatory comment and poured fuel on to a fast-growing national rebellion which eventually resulted in more than 25 million summonses across the country being issued for non-payment and was a key factor in the Tory coup which forced the resignation of Mrs Thatcher as prime minister in November 1990.

The *Coventry Evening Telegraph*'s editorial policy with regard to the poll tax was to oppose the unfairness of a flat-rate charge for all, regardless of circumstances, but also to condemn protesters like Dave Nellist who said they were prepared to break the law by refusing to pay. There was nothing very unusual about taking such a position for most if not all regional newspapers instinctively felt they should not support law-breaking, yet as things turned out it was the lawbreakers who scored a resounding victory in the end. The magistrates' courts system across England and Wales simply could not cope with an unprecedented avalanche of work. As a result, Mrs Thatcher was ousted as prime minister in November 1990 by her own Tory MPs to be replaced by John Major who promptly scrapped the community charge and introduced the council tax in its place.

Housing committee chairman John Mutton, who went on to become council leader, became the first Coventry city councillor to state publicly that he would not pay the "unfair" poll tax, complaining that his last rates bill had been £430 compared with £1,600 for his family's community charge payments. I reported this and the *Evening Telegraph* questioned the example Mutton was setting for thousands of people living in council housing, with the headline: "If our housing chief won't pay up, why should the tenants?"

Mutton's protest was, in theory, a futile gesture since the council would have been forced to obtain a court order to deduct poll tax payments from his wage as a Co-op Dairy milkman. But the point about the poll tax rebellion across England was that the sheer scale of the uprising – the biggest civil disobedience campaign of the 20th century, with multiple summonses for 25 million people, getting on for half of the entire adult population – meant the judicial system simply would have taken many years to deal with all of the non-payers.

Significantly, the anti-poll tax campaign took off all over the country and was not simply confined to poorer areas. There were riots in London and even in the genteel Tory stronghold of Tunbridge Wells in Kent, one-third of electors weren't paying the new charge. While Labour would not admit it at the time, it is impossible today to deny Militant's claim to have defeated the poll tax, and hounded Mrs Thatcher from office, through direct action.

While nowhere near the same scale as the poll tax rebellion, the government's decision in 1989 to privatise the water authorities attracted plenty of opposition from Labour and left-wing protest groups who believed the provision of something as basic as water should be in public rather than private hands. The newly privatised Severn Trent Water had a flamboyant chair called John Bellak who by the time he took early retirement in 1994 was being paid £230,000 a year (equivalent to £443,000 today). Bellak was a natural media performer, always happy talking to journalists, and his first wheeze was to get rid of foreign bottled water at board meetings, which he had replaced by Severn Trent's finest straight from the tap while happily posing for press pictures glugging back the product he was being paid so handsomely to promote.

Bellak's line on fast-rising water bills was that the publicly-owned water authorities had presided over decades of under-investment in infrastructure. Cities like Birmingham and Coventry, for example, were still relying on Victorian pipes and sewers which were in desperate need of replacement but the cost of modernisation would be huge, hence customers had to pay more for their water. This was also the official government position.

One battle the water companies did not win though concerned a move to install water meters in all houses, thereby getting rid of water rates and charging consumers according to the amount of water used. The idea, the Labour party claimed, would have hit large families in the pocket while leaving single and two-person households better off.

Chapter Twenty-Four

My Posh Colleagues

O ne of the oddities of the *Coventry Telegraph* in the mid-1980s was that the editorial floor had a plentiful supply of young men who had attended public schools. It was rumoured that the paper had operated an unofficial policy to hire only candidates from independent schools, with job application forms divided into two piles – public school applicants, and the rest. The state school pile, it was said, would be thrown into the nearest bin.

Many of the recruits from public schools arrived just before I joined the paper under the supervision of deputy editor John Cross, an odd man renowned for extreme parsimony which even extended to saving money by making his own suits and shoes. Cross was also notorious for refusing mileage expenses claims from reporters, arguing the toss about the distance between Coventry and Warwick, for example.

There was much speculation that Cross, who retired just before I joined the *CET*, preferred privately educated candidates to those from state schools. I do not know whether there was any truth in this. Perhaps the claim was no more than an urban myth, although allegations about the *CET* being a feeder paper for public schools were widespread among journalists at other Warwickshire newspapers.

Geoff Elliott is adamant that the *Evening Telegraph* did not go out with the intention of recruiting from public schools. He told me: "We set out to recruit the best three postgraduates each year. We didn't care where they came from. We went to a great deal of trouble to choose the right ones. It didn't matter how long they stayed. Nobody in journalism stays very long. Our responsibility was to bring into journalism the best people."

I find his assertion that 'nobody in journalism stays very long' to be a little world-weary, cynical even. My experience, certainly during the 1980s and 1990s, was that a great many journalists spent their working lives pretty much with one company and the job for life theme was of course deeply embedded at the *Coventry Evening Telegraph* – embodied by the 21 Club for long-serving employees. Some trainees, of course, moved on fairly quickly once they had qualified, but the newsroom was populated by senior reporters and subs who had been on the paper for many years.

Whether the abundance of recruits from public schools was deliberate or not, it was undeniably the case when I arrived in 1986 that the newsroom was populated with plenty of privately educated men and punctuated by a certain braying oafishness, with shouts of "where's me fag?" commonplace.

The zenith, surely, of the *Evening Telegraph*'s dalliance with public schools was the decision shortly after I started to hire Roland Watson, who had been at Eton and captained the school cricket team in the annual match against Harrow at Lord's. Watson, one of the more talented journalists I've ever worked with, would have been a splendid addition to any newsroom. He went on to become political editor and then foreign editor of *The Times*.

Another young recruit from public school was Jeremy Vine, the BBC news presenter, who was educated at Epsom College and joined the paper from Durham University as a trainee. Vine didn't last very long at the *Telegraph*, leaving in 1987, little more than a year after joining, to take up a place a place on the BBC's training scheme after being given permission to break his indentures with the full backing of Geoff Elliott.

Vine touches on the oddities of the *Evening Telegraph* in his autobiography, in particular the news-editing skills of Geoff Grimmer. Having returned from covering the magistrates court one day, Vine was confident of having written a good story with the introductory paragraph explaining how a man had walked up to a woman and demanded sex. Grimmer declared this was not a good 'intro' since there was nothing unusual about a man wanting sex – we all did.

The 1980s and early 1990s turned out to be a golden era for the *Coventry Telegraph* in terms of producing talented journalists, many of them hired by Geoff Elliott. As well as Vine and Watson, the political desk boasted Joe Murphy and David Cracknell, both of whom trained under me. Murphy is now political editor at the *London Evening Standard*, while Cracknell moved into public relations after a long period as political editor of the *Sunday Times*. Michael Prescott, who was a trainee at the *Coventry Telegraph* and left the paper in 1986, also became political editor of the *Sunday Times*. The *Coventry Telegraph-Sunday Times* link also worked for Andrew Grice, who left the *Evening Telegraph* shortly before I started and became political editor at the *Sunday Times*. He is now on the *Independent*. David Brindle, public services editor at *The Guardian*, was political editor at the *Coventry Evening Telegraph* in the early 1980s. Dermot Murnaghan, the Sky TV News presenter, was a *Coventry Evening Telegraph* trainee in the early 1980s.

Trainees like Vine generally started their career by working for the *Telegraph*'s weekly free *Coventry Citizen* newspaper under the wing of its eccentric editor Barry Clark, whose flimsy spectacles were forever held together with pieces of Sellotape long before Coronation Street scriptwriters thought of the idea for Jack Duckworth, and whose propensity for falling over after leaving various pubs late at night was legendary. Clark was the proud holder of the Scouting Association's Silver Acorn award. He had an addiction to sugar in his tea resulting in the loss of most of his teeth by the time he was 50, a braying laugh, drank copious amounts of beer in the Town Wall, and was generally surrounded in the pub by a coterie of good-looking young men who would discuss subjects such as how to cook a cassoulet or the forthcoming Edinburgh Festival. How much knowledge of journalism Barry ever imparted to young trainees is another matter, but he would certainly have given them a run for their money in the beer-drinking stakes.

Laddish behaviour was par for the course at the *Telegraph* in 1986 and sexist comments were generally ignored by managers, although this has to be seen in the context of what was deemed acceptable behaviour in the workplace, at least by men, a quarter of a century ago.

One male colleague seemed to be obsessed with attempting to work out whether any of his colleagues might be gay. He would declare in a loud voice: "Research suggests ten percent of the population are homosexual. Now, there are about twenty men in the office at the moment, so that means two are homosexual. Well, it's not me, so who are they?" The word 'homosexual' would roll around his mouth and be spat out with distaste as if it had about seven syllables.

I should say here that Geoff Elliott does not accept my recollection of sexism, or 'misogyny' as he puts it. We shall have to agree to disagree on that point. I don't seek to claim the *Coventry Telegraph* was any more discriminatory than other newspaper office in the Midlands at that time, but I certainly recall an atmosphere that was decidedly macho where female reporters were considered by some men as good for only two things – writing soft features or providing love interest for the boys.

Gradually, as we approached the 1990s, the paper began to recruit more women reporters and women also found themselves promoted to junior roles on the newsdesk. Even so, there was still plenty of testosterone flying about, which sometimes escaped from the newsroom with unfortunate consequences. Five-a-side football matches that we played under floodlights at Tile Hill occasionally descended into minor thuggery, with one memorable occasion enlivened by a senior editorial executive who considered he'd been badly fouled chasing a political reporter around the pitch, fists waving furiously, screaming: "Do you want some of this, eh, do you?"

Two of my female colleagues disclosed that they were pointedly asked at their job interview whether they had a boyfriend or husband and if they were intending to start a family. I'm not certain that line of questioning was fair even 30 years ago.

A female colleague, who landed a trainee reporter job at the *CET* when she was 19, recalled:

"I remember my interview day in 1987 vividly. I was on the NCTJ journalism course in Cardiff where males and females were treated equally and well, and I was rather innocent of the fact that in many places we were still in the 1970s.

"I was interviewed first by Geoff Elliott, who asked me if I had a boyfriend, and I said no, and he said women usually lost interest in work when they got married. He showed me a copy of a previous day's paper which included a picture of a model, topless and on horseback riding through Coventry as Lady Godiva. He asked me what I thought of it and should he have published it – I said I thought it was acceptable as a one off if the story explained the context but that obviously you wouldn't print pictures like that regularly in a family paper – what was I meant to say?

"Then I was interviewed by the news editor, who asked me if I had a boyfriend. I said no, but he then continued regardless and said they found that when they took on girls, they usually went off and got married and had babies after a couple of years and weren't interested any more and the paper had wasted time and money training them, and was I going to do that?

"It was a bit odd, seeing as I'd said I didn't have a boyfriend, but I said no, I had no intention of doing that and I was serious about pursuing a career in journalism. I remember being really shocked as we'd talked about interviews on my course, and about questions that might come up and we'd never even thought of this area of questioning."

Casual, and not so casual, sexist attitudes were pretty commonplace at the *CET* in the early 1980s. A few years before I arrived the sports desk amused itself by organising an annual 'Bird of the Building' competition where men voted to select the best-looking female employee. It was an initiative of such gross insensitivity that it wouldn't have looked out of place in the TV sit-com *On the Buses*. A 'Gay Board' featuring suggestive photos and explicit postcards sent from holidays, another sports desk initiative, lingered on into the 2000s before being removed in preparation for a visit from Trinity Mirror chief executive Sly Bailey.

Chapter Twenty-Five

MPs and a Charm Offensive

My first few weeks in Coventry had to be devoted to a charm offensive as I sought to placate politicians who were upset by the *Telegraph*'s coverage of Coventry council and Warwickshire County Council. To be fair to the editor, he recognised that bridges needed to be built and that the appointment of a new political editor represented a chance to start afresh, so he provided me with a list of politicians whose egos would have to be massaged. As I examined the piece of paper it dawned on me that I'd be having some difficult conversations with plenty of Coventry and Warwickshire councillors and MPs, most of whom were furious at being humiliated by *Peeping Tom*.

Almost all of the key Coventry council committee chairmen were wary of dealing with the paper and the council leader, Peter Lister, appeared not the slightest bit interested in forming a relationship with us although perhaps that had more to do with his own personality. The *Guardian* newspaper obituary on Lister in 2002 quoted one of his successors as Coventry council leader, Nick Nolan: "Peter was difficult with his opponents and impossible with his friends. He had incredible intellectual clarity and made enormous demands on himself and others. He was also a man of puritanical integrity, not at all interested in the trappings of power." All I can say is that Lister was stand-offish and uncommunicative whenever I tried to engage him in conversation, but perhaps he just didn't like journalists, and he certainly made it abundantly clear he didn't like the *Coventry Evening Telegraph*.

It has become fashionable in recent years for politicians from the left to blame the media for the Labour Party's failure to win general elections, with the inference that newspapers somehow conspire to persuade their readers, who clearly cannot think for themselves, to vote Conservative. I can only speak for regional newspapers and wish to make it clear that I was never asked by any editor or news editor during my 14 years at the *Coventry Evening Telegraph* and 11 years at *The Birmingham Post* to take a particular political stance when writing a news story, nor would I have done so.

While researching this book I came across an extraordinary memo written in the early 1980s by a senior *CET* journalist. The document drills down into the heart of Coventry and Warwickshire's key political figures at the time, exposing their frailties and prejudices, and makes it clear that the *Evening Telegraph* was disliked equally by Labour and the Conservatives, which I suppose shows that the paper was at least even-handed in its approach.

The memo, which was drawn up to give some tips to a new political editor in the early 1980s (not me), describes one Coventry MP as an "intensely likeable buffoon" while another, long since dead, was said to be "deeply ambitious" but with a "dodgy marriage". Jim Pawsey, Tory MP for Rugby and Kenilworth, was described as a "right wing rent-a-quote Catholic". In fact, Pawsey hailed from a working-class background, was educated at Coventry Technical College. While he liked to give the impression of being a Thatcherite on the right of the Conservative party, the truth was rather more complex and I would have classed him as fairly mainstream. He chaired the backbench Tory education committee in the House of Commons for a number of years and resisted attempts by colleagues on the right to introduce education vouchers, a move that would have cut dramatically the cost to working class parents of sending their children to an independent school. When I asked him to explain his thinking, he said he feared vouchers would prompt a stampede to take children out of badly-performing schools, which would result in the schools delivering ever poorer results and eventually facing closure, which would in turn put impossible demands on local education authorities.

Sir Dudley Smith, the former Tory MP for Warwick and Leamington, was described in the memo as "a bloody useless constituency MP", and as someone who hated the *CET* which he regarded as a left-wing rag. Sir Dudley went down in *CET* folklore after a mix-up in his office resulted in the MP mistakenly sending an abusive note to a constituent. The error involved a woman who continually wrote to Sir Dudley complaining about this, that and the other. Sir Dudley sent a note to his office along the lines of "make the usual reply and get this bloody woman off my back". Unfortunately, a flustered secretary sent Sir Dudley's angry note to the woman rather than a standard letter, with the result that the furious constituent forwarded the missive to the *Evening Telegraph*, much to the newspaper's delight.

Peter Lister was said in the memo to be someone "likely to bite your head off for no reason at all" and was hemmed in by a "dynasty mafia" in the Coventry Labour group, which was about right. The new political editor was advised, as I was a few years later, to take "a new leaf" stance by promising both Labour and the Tories that a fresh approach was to be taken with regard to political reporting.

During my first week Geoff Elliott asked me to drive out to Birdingbury, near Rugby, to conduct a charm offensive with John Vereker, the leader of the Conservative group on Warwickshire County Council, who had fallen out with the *Evening Telegraph*. The Conservatives had controlled the county council for decades, but lost power to a minority Labour-led administration in 1985 during a period that saw the cost of delivering local government services rise dramatically. Household rates bills in the county rose by 20 percent in 1985 and 10 percent a year later.

The Tories did not take the 1985 election result well. When all of the votes had been counted there were 26 Conservative councillors, 24 Labour, 10 Liberals and one Independent. As the *Coventry Evening Telegraph* gleefully pointed out, the Conservatives had managed to lose overall control of the county for the first time in 96 years. Vereker, as leader of the largest group, in an astonishing display of ineptitude veering on arrogance, attempted to carry on as normal, telling the *Telegraph* that nothing would change, the Tories as the largest party would continue to run the council and would simply have to consult more with the other parties.

John Vereker hailed from a famous army family and invariably wore a regimental tie. He was a descendant of Lord Gort, who commanded the ill-fated British Expeditionary Force in France in 1940, and was not a man given to taking personal criticism from newspapers lightly. A difficult meeting at his house gave him an opportunity to lecture me for an hour with regard to the supposed shortcomings of the *Coventry Evening Telegraph*.

Vereker was particularly upset at the *Telegraph*'s editorial campaign opposing cuts in council services brought about by the Conservative government's public spending squeeze. He argued that there had been no cuts at all since the total amount of Government grant allocated to the council had increased year by year. This was true, up to a point. But of course, the increase was significantly below inflation and therefore a cut in real terms. We agreed that in future when I was writing about the county council's finances I would explain that the cuts in question were 'real terms reductions'. This appeared to satisfy him and our relationship was relatively cordial thereafter.

Chapter Twenty-Six

'Crusty Bill' and Lord Mayors

In common with most councils, Coventry's Lord Mayor was chosen on a 'Buggin's turn' principle. Generally, the longest serving city councillor who had not yet been mayor was gifted the job, and for years Labour refused to allow the Conservatives to get their hands on the mayoralty at all. From 1979 to 1996 Coventry had 17 Labour Lord Mayors and only one Conservative. The reasons for Labour failing to share out the much sought-after position more equitably were lost in the mists of time, but what is certain is that most councillors regarded becoming mayor as the peak of their career and would do almost anything to spend a year basking in the glory of being first citizen. If their turn could be speeded up by denying the role to a rival political party then so be it was very much the view taken by Labour in Coventry.

The obvious problem with choosing mayors on a time-served basis is that the person selected isn't necessarily the best candidate for the job. Over the years I've come to the firm conclusion that it is impossible to predict how someone will perform when they become a mayor or lord mayor and, most importantly, are given the keys to the civic cocktail cabinet. Some candidates who I was certain would be excellent mayors were simply awful, turning into pompous autocrats under the weight of the office. Others who I'd imagined would be terrible and unable to communicate with the public suddenly became popular leaders and displayed a touchy-feely manner that had hitherto not been apparent. I recall one deputy lord mayor whose fondness for the bottle was such that the *Evening Telegraph* felt obliged to inform the council privately that such conduct would be exposed in the newspaper unless something was done. The warning worked and the deputy mayor became, if not a model of sobriety, a much-reformed character.

The Lord Mayor of Coventry from 1985-1986 was Bill McKernan, a veteran Scottish Labour councillor who was dubbed 'Crusty Bill' by *Peeping Tom* because of his alleged short temper. This was a little unfair for Bill was a good lord mayor and any crustiness on his part was generally reserved for journalists because Bill, along with most of his party colleagues, regarded the media with suspicion. Born at the end of the First World War, Bill was a veteran of the Labour movement and prone to name-dropping when it suited him. "As I said to Clem (Attlee)", was a comment he would throw into a conversation every so often.

The fact that Bill liked a drink was no secret. A member of my political reporting team at Coventry, Len Freeman, recalls being sent to interview the Lord Mayor at 9.30 in the morning. Bill's first words were: "You'll have a drink?" Not wishing to appear rude or ungrateful Freeman agreed and was handed a gin and tonic that consisted almost wholly of gin and the merest whiff of tonic water that had been languishing in the drinks cabinet for so long it had lost any fizz that it might once have had. Bill poured himself a similarly rocket-fueled G&T and they both drank up. Then they had another. Freeman, no slouch himself at drinking, staggered back to the office in some disarray.

I had a drink with Bill McKernan an hour or so before he was due to welcome a Japanese government minister to Coventry, the first such visit since the Second World War. The council, fearing possible protests, had put a lot of effort into generating positive media coverage and persuading citizens to put all thoughts of Japan's conduct in the war behind them by stressing Coventry's reputation as a city of reconciliation. I explained to Bill that the visit would be difficult for me personally as my father fought in the Far East during the war and knew all about Japanese brutality during the conflict.

Bill sank his drink, looked at me and said: "Aye lad, I know. I can't stand the bastards either, but we've just got to go through with this." We toasted my father with another drink. Or it may have been another couple.

Shortly after starting at the *CET* I was invited to a council reception and dinner attended by the great and good of Coventry. Proudly armed with new business cards I set about introducing myself to as many people as possible. Almost every Labour councillor I met had the same story – they neither liked nor trusted the 'Tory Telegraph'. However, most said they were prepared to give me a chance. But this rapprochement did not extend to former lord mayor and council leader Arthur Waugh, one of Labour's leading lights during the post-war redevelopment of Coventry. Waugh, always known as Arthur Waugh Senior or Big Arthur, to distinguish him from his councillor son, also Arthur, known as Arthur Waugh Junior, or Little Arthur, sat next to me at dinner. "Who'd you say you were?", he asked. Waugh Snr studied my business card closely, turned to me and said: "Evening Telegraph eh? I'll never fucking well speak to you again". He was as good as his word and ignored me for the rest of his life.

Chapter Twenty-Seven

Party Conferences and Dodgy Laptops

My arrival at Coventry coincided with the introduction of new technology into the news room following an agreement between management and the National Union of Journalists to replace typewriters with fairly primitive word processors, handing a significant pay rise to journalists in return for their willingness to embrace change.

In a stunning example of the way in which naïve newspaper managers were duped by the fast-growing ICT industry, the *Telegraph* managed to spend a considerable amount of money purchasing early versions of laptops that rarely, if ever, worked properly. These bulky pieces of kit were supposed to enable stories to be 'sent down the line' by plugging telephone receivers into the laptop's docking station, but the slightest interference on the line brought communication to an abrupt halt.

The system was rendered completely useless by the introduction of domestic trim phones, which could not be plugged into the laptops. This meant reporters out on the road had to search for telephone boxes where old-style receivers were still in use. But there was another problem. Inserting money into the box when a call was answered resulted in the laptop connection being broken. Whether anyone on the paper tested this equipment before signing a cheque was unclear, but if someone did do so it clearly wasn't a journalist up against a deadline and attempting to file copy from a public call box on a cold and windswept Blackpool promenade.

I joined the *Coventry Evening Telegraph* in September 1986, two weeks before the start of the party conference season. Geoff Elliott had been insistent during my interview on two things – I would be expected to attend the Labour and Conservative conferences each year, and I would write a punchy political column for the paper to be published weekly.

First up was Labour at Blackpool in a gathering remembered for the expulsion of Liverpool city council deputy leader Derek Hatton over his membership of Militant. Hatton and his supporters arrived at the conference in a fleet of taxis pursued by television film crews, but the publicity could not save him. Labour members overwhelmingly approved the expulsion in a closed session and the decision was widely applauded in the conference hall.

Neil Kinnock, who a year earlier had used his leader's conference speech at Bournemouth to deliver a damning condemnation of Militant and Hatton's influence on Liverpool city council, was beginning the long process of making Labour electable again following a collapse in support under Michael Foot. Five years later, the hard-left's influence suffered another severe blow when Coventry south-east MP Dave Nellist was expelled for being a member of Militant.

My first visit to Blackpool was a huge culture shock since I'd never been north of Coventry and holidays as a boy were always taken in genteel resorts in Devon and Cornwall or the Isle of Wight. Driving into the town on the Sunday morning I'd never seen so many people in one place. There appeared to be a pub or a bar every 100 yards illuminated by garish neon lights and the streets were overflowing with day-trippers, holidaymakers and revellers who were there to see the illuminations and were determined to enjoy themselves, making it impossible to drive safely at any more than a snail's pace.

The hotel I was staying in had been booked by the news desk secretary before I moved to Coventry and was, I later discovered, where my predecessor Andrew Evans had stayed when the conference was last in Blackpool. The only thing that could be said in its favour was its location, next to the Winter Gardens conference centre. The building rather summed up Blackpool – cheap and run down. Single bedrooms were barely larger than a prison cell and the walls were paper thin. The shabby hotel was also the base for reporters from the Labour-supporting *Guardian* newspaper although, I was amused to discover, not by the paper's executives who lorded it by staying up the road with Neil Kinnock and the shadow cabinet at the four-star conference hotel, The Imperial.

The first challenge was to charge my troublesome laptop on the faint chance that it might work and I would be able to send some stories over to Coventry. A frantic search of the bedroom for a plug socket proved fruitless. No sign of a connection behind the bed or the wardrobe or in the bathroom. The hotel manager simply laughed when I asked about an electricity supply: "A power socket? Blimey, no. We'd have people bringing in heaters and God knows what if we put sockets in the bedrooms." He did however generously agree to charge my laptop using his own personal electricity supply, at no extra cost.

Geoff Grimmer had drummed into me the importance of liberally sprinkling quotes from Coventry and Warwickshire delegates into my stories. Readers wanted to know what local people were doing and saying at the conference and their views on the big issues of the day, he claimed, although the truth almost certainly was that the average *Evening Telegraph* reader couldn't have cared less about party conferences, or what the Coventry delegates thought about anything.

All Labour delegates were allocated a dedicated seat in the Winter Gardens and the names and seat numbers of occupants were published in the conference handbook, making it easy to track down representatives from our patch. Carefully checking the seating arrangements, I positioned myself at the end of a row in which a prominent Coventry union official was sitting. Gesticulating wildly with my hands, I mouthed at him in a stage whisper: "It's the *Coventry Telegraph*. Can I have a word please?" After a long delay the man finally shuffled along to the end of the row towards where I was standing. It immediately became obvious that the attractions of the Winter Gardens' many bars, open from ten in the morning, meant I wouldn't be getting any pearls of wisdom for my story from him. I'd scarcely seen a drunker person, sweating profusely, incapable of speaking, and barely able to stand up. So much for local quotes.

There were, though, some pluses attached to visiting Blackpool. Robert's Oyster Bar on the promenade, for example, as well as the world-famous Yates's Wine Lodge, a lunchtime haunt for the likes of author and journalist Keith Waterhouse and his Fleet Street pals who contented themselves with regular top-ups from the bar's unique draught champagne tap.

The Conservative conference the following week at Bournemouth was expected to be a somewhat difficult occasion for the *Evening Telegraph* thanks to the behaviour a year previously of my predecessor as political editor, Andrew Evans. The Tory conference in 1985 was at Blackpool, a year after the 1984 conference in Brighton at which Irish terrorists attempted to assassinate Margaret Thatcher and her cabinet by bombing the Grand Hotel. As a result, security for the 1985 gathering was especially tight with body searches for delegates and the press as well as airport-style scanners.

Evans proceeded through security and, having been searched and cleared to enter the Winter Gardens, inexplicably produced a cigar from his jacket pocket, waved it about, and announced: "You didn't find my exploding cigar, then". Security staff and police were not amused. Evans was detained and questioned, although eventually allowed in to the conference, and the Tories submitted a complaint to Geoff Elliott who feared the *Telegraph* might be banned from attending the 1986 conference. In the end a pass was granted, but Geoff Elliott warned me the cigar incident might be mentioned and I could expect a thorough search from security. There was no mention of a cigar when I arrived at security, but the search was certainly thorough.

My first experiences of the party conference season were made tolerable by the unflagging generosity of the Scotch Whisky Association, which always has a stand in the exhibition hall at the main political gatherings. The association's aim is simple enough: to try to persuade MPs whose party is in government to campaign for tax on whisky sales to be reduced, thereby boosting exports and the Scottish economy, and of course boosting the profits of the distillers. MPs from the opposition party are lobbied just as hard in case they might form the next government.

The time-honoured custom was for journalists to make their way to the Scotch Whisky Association stand in the conference exhibition area and engage staff in conversation, which inevitably led to the issue of the iniquitous tax on alcohol. Provided you were prepared to stand and be lectured for a few minutes, nodding sympathetically in the right places, a prized ticket for the association's Scotch Whisky reception would be handed over with a suggestion that "if you're not doing anything tomorrow night, we'd be happy to give you a drink or two".

Drinks receptions at the party conferences, at lunchtime and in the evening, represent a chink of light at the end of a very long and dark tunnel for journalists who have to cover the political events. Some of these gatherings are tolerable, others not so tolerable, but most offer free food and drinks for hungry and thirsty hacks. However, the Scotch Whisky Association reception, essentially two hours devoted to sampling as much free malt whisky as possible, is in a class of its own and naturally attracts huge numbers of MPs, government ministers, and shadow ministers. I spotted Ken Clarke knocking back the Macallan's when he was Chancellor, but he wasn't inclined to sing for his supper and didn't cut whisky taxes in his next budget.

Attending Conservative conferences towards the end of the 1980s and the beginning of the 1990s I realised for the first time the extent of ill feeling, hatred even, that existed among the Tory grassroots members and also among many MPs for the European Union. It was clear even then that the growing power of the EU and its influence over UK laws and courts was a matter that threatened to split the Conservative party down the middle, as both John Major and latterly David Cameron found to their cost. Many Tory members I spoke to, not all elderly, held an extraordinary view of the UK and truly believed Britain was still a world power able to trade anywhere across the globe as it saw fit. The fact that this country had lost an empire, had been bankrupted by the war, bailed out militarily and financially by America, utterly humiliated and exposed as a non-world power by the Suez Crisis did not dawn on these people for a second. Sadly, many of the most vociferous anti-EU Tories based their views on simply not caring very much for foreigners.

It was at a Tory conference towards the end of the 1980s where I witnessed first-hand the antipathy felt by many Conservative members to pro-European ministers. I was at a reception given by the West Midlands Conservative Association when the Europhile Foreign Secretary Sir Geoffrey Howe and his wife Elspeth walked in to be greeted by hissing and audible stage whispers of: "Here come the socialists." A year or so later Sir Geoffrey, by now deputy prime minister, resigned from the Government and triggered the events that led to Mrs Thatcher's downfall with a blistering House of Commons speech in which he accused the prime minister of doing her best to 'subvert' the UK's membership of the European Union and, quoting Harold Macmillan's wise words, warned his anti-EU colleagues against Britain 'retreating into a ghetto of sentimentality about our past'.

In his speech, Sir Geoffrey said: "The Prime Minister's perceived attitude towards Europe is running increasingly serious risks for the future of our nation. It risks minimising our influence and maximising our chances of being once again shut out."

In a moment of great House of Commons drama, he ended with a stark challenge to Tory MPs: "The time has come for others to consider their own response to the tragic conflict of loyalties, with which I myself have wrestled for perhaps too long." Days later, Margaret Thatcher was out of office, savagely ousted by Tory MPs, and was replaced by John Major.

The mid-1990s saw a concerted effort by Members of the European Parliament (MEPs) to get local newspapers interested in writing about their work in Brussels. The European authorities and the British government, perhaps wary of looming trouble over the Maastricht Treaty and the expansion of the EU, had created a cash fund to enable MEPs to take regional journalists to Brussels and Strasbourg to witness first-hand the work of the EU parliament.

I went several times to both cities courtesy of Coventry and Warwickshire MEPs and it quickly became clear to me that the EU lifestyle could easily suck in even the most militant Eurosceptic. Lavish expenses, superb restaurants, first class travel and no-cost-spared modern parliamentary buildings naturally appealed to MEPs and journalists alike. Some of the Coventry and Warwickshire Conservative MEPs were openly hostile to Britain's membership of the EU, arguing that we had joined an economic community not a political clique with powers to set and oversee British laws. Nevertheless, they put themselves forward for election to a parliament they fundamentally disagreed with, and it seemed to me they were more than comfortable with the Brussels-Strasbourg lifestyle where boozy lunches were often followed by equally boozy dinners.

The *Evening Telegraph*'s commitment to political coverage was such that I headed a four-person desk, with two political reporters and an education correspondent. This was a sizeable contingent compared with other regional evening papers and in addition at busy times we'd be assigned a trainee reporter to help out. It was made clear a significant part of my role would be to form close contacts with the leading political figures in Coventry and Warwickshire and that this would involve a certain amount of wining and dining, at the company's expense of course.

Part of the job involved regular trips to Westminster, where a lobby pass allowed access to the Houses of Parliament and enabled me to attend Downing Street Government briefings. Although things have changed a bit now, in the 1980s and 1990s journalists in parliament enjoyed considerable benefits including a subsidised press restaurant where hacks and MPs consumed high-quality meals washed down with bottles of cut-price vintage wine from the House of Commons' renowned cellar. There was also a press bar and a well-stocked library complete with comfortable leather armchairs in which journalists tired after their lunch-time excesses would sometimes snooze away the hours before tea.

Chapter Twenty-Eight

Wining and Dining

C oventry in the late 1980s was certainly not a promising place for cuisine. The Town Wall, although a super pub, was not a suitable venue to treat a councillor or MP to lunch. The bar space was cramped, the menu was pretty much limited to burgers or sausage batches, you'd be lucky to find a seat after 12.30, and if you did find a seat it would be difficult to converse with a guest given the crescendo of drink-fuelled noise and general mayhem surrounding you.

Carl's restaurant in Lower Holyhead Road, conveniently close to the *Evening Telegraph* offices, was an all-too brief shining light in the early 1990s, dispensing dishes such as home-made terrine with brioche and medallions of pork in a Roquefort sauce. But Carl's food proved too rich for the good folk of Coventry, and the custom provided by *Evening Telegraph* journalists entertaining their contacts was not enough to keep the restaurant in business.

Corks wine bar off Gosford Street close to the Council House became the political desk's favourite location for entertaining since it boasted a decent wine list and menu. It was the place where I caused some unintentional hilarity by telling the owner he was under-charging for a bottle of La Cour Pavillion which I had paid more for in France than in Coventry. The next time we went, the price of the wine had been increased much to the amusement of my colleagues. That didn't put us off going to Corks several times a week, and the Militant Tendency supporters of Dave Nellist certainly didn't object to regular visits to take food and drink from the capitalist press in return for the titbits of political gossip they were able to give us.

For special occasions, usually when someone else was picking up the bill, there was Quo Vadis, an Italian restaurant in Barker Butts Lane, but a better bet to my mind was Lino's on the eastern outskirts of Coventry close to Coombe Abbey Country Park. Lino's was a unique proposition in Coventry, popular with Coventry City footballers, trade union officials, businessmen on expense accounts, and was certainly one of the most expensive places in the area to eat. It was a favourite spot for Geoffrey Robinson, the wealthy Labour MP for Coventry North-west. Lino and his wife had been in charge of catering at Coventry City Football Club before setting up their own restaurant in 1985.

Robinson was on the board at the football club and would certainly have used his influence to put a bit of trade Lino's way by talking up the delights of what was for a number of years arguably Coventry's premier eating place.

Some people might have described Lino's as a tad pretentious, or possibly a bit theatrical. There was a permanent whiff from gas-powered burners as bow-tied chefs with exaggerated foreign accents flambéd French-style dishes at the table, sending flames shooting up towards the ceiling as cognac was liberally thrown about. There was a great sense of drama about the place which boasted an extensive wine list, famously offering one bottle at £1,000. Whether the bottle actually existed was a matter of keen debate among my colleagues, but no one dared risk ordering it to find out. I strongly suspect that even the *Evening Telegraph*'s generous expenses regime at the time wouldn't have stretched to paying a grand for a bottle of wine.

Evening Telegraph restaurant critics over the years, including me, were not over-impressed with Lino's, often pointing out that the quality of the food was high but so were the prices being charged. The restaurant's owner, Gomez Lino, rarely missed an opportunity to write to the editor or the managing director complaining that a critical review in the Evening Telegraph had resulted in a fall-off in customers and he was losing money as a result. He was routinely ignored.

Chapter Twenty-Nine

1987 General Election

Going into the 1987 General Election, three of Coventry's four parliamentary constituencies were held by Labour and one, Coventry south-west, by Conservative John Butcher. The Tories had high hopes of winning Coventry north-west and Coventry south-east, but both seats were easily held by Labour with Geoffrey Robinson recording a 5,563-vote majority in the north-west, and Dave Nellist winning by 6,653 votes in the south-east.

Labour's candidate in Coventry south-west, Bob Slater, was a poor choice. A college lecturer from Leicester, he turned out to be an uninspiring campaigner, very ill at ease with the media, who often avoided answering questions by complaining that he was being asked to comment on matters that were the responsibility of Coventry city councillors rather than an MP in Westminster. *Peeping Tom* brilliantly dubbed Slater 'See You Later Slater'.

He was no match for the savvy and quotable Butcher whose good looks were compared by his supporters to the film star Robert Redford and who it was whispered would be using 'American-style' canvassing methods to drill down at street level and target disillusioned Labour voters. No one ever bottomed out what the American tactics were, and I doubt whether they ever existed, but Butcher won the seat fairly convincingly with a majority of 3,210. The result might have been very different were it not for the efforts of Coventry city councillor Rob Wheway, for many years the sole Liberal on the city council, who took a credible 20 percent of the votes cast. Labour, clearly having learned nothing from 1987, reselected Slater to stand in Coventry south-west at the 1992 General Election, where he again lost to Butcher although he did reduce the Tory majority to 1,436.

The election campaign was a busy time for me and the politics desk, not least because my wife was heavily pregnant with our first child, James, who would be born a week before polling day. There was no such thing then as paternity leave, and anyway I couldn't have justified taking time off so close to the election. After the election Geoff Elliott kindly wrote to thank me for my professionalism, but added: "I'm not sure your wife would see it that way."

Before social media existed, the three main parties felt the need to hold early morning press briefings in Coventry hoping to grab the local news agenda for the day ahead. Prominent MPs, ministers and shadow ministers would be shipped in to boost the standing of local candidates.

Despite the best efforts of the political parties, there were no shock results in the *Coventry Evening Telegraph* circulation area, although the gritty former pit town of Nuneaton did rather surprisingly return Conservative candidate Lew Stevens, an unremarkable middle-aged pipe-smoking rugby-supporting local businessman who gave every indication of having strolled out of the 1950s.

Stevens initially won the seat in 1983 after Les Huckfield, the Labour MP for Nuneaton since 1967, decided to seek a safer constituency and did not put himself forward for reselection. Huckfield had been tipped to be the candidate in the rock-solid safe Labour seat of Sedgefield, but local party members selected a young barrister by the name of Tony Blair instead. For the 1987 General Election Labour selected Valerie Veness to contest Nuneaton. Veness was an Islington friend of Jeremy Corbyn and was every bit to the left as Huckfield if not more so and quite unsuited to campaigning in a place like Nuneaton.

She gained national notoriety for allegedly having said a number of years previously: "A Labour government has got to take on the people who obstruct it, arresting them if necessary, arm the workers if necessary." It wasn't the type of sentiment likely to go down very well with working class communities in the Midlands. In the end Stevens took 45 percent of the vote and won with a majority of 5,665. I was at his victory party at the Coton Chilvers Conservative Club in Nuneaton along with the Tory faithful who couldn't quite believe their man had won for a second time. Labour didn't make the same selection mistake for the 1992 General Election when they chose Bill Olner, an ex-car worker and safe pair of hands. A popular former mayor of Nuneaton, Olner defeated Stevens by 1,631 votes and held the seat until he retired in 2010.

Bill, in common with most of the Warwickshire MPs, had a reasonably good relationship with the *Coventry Evening Telegraph* and was always willing to be quoted on matters of local and national interest. I used to give him lunch at the Labour party conference each year. Somewhat annoyingly, he would always insist on a fillet steak, 'very well done', which was inevitably the most expensive item on the menu and generally raised news desk questions about the size of my expenses. One year, when we were at Blackpool, I scoured the town for a restaurant that did not offer fillet steak and thought I had found the very place, a rather small down-at-heel Italian 'ristorante' down a side street. Bill gazed intently at the menu, looking up and down several times at the list of various pizzas and pastas, but could not see the dish he desired. Beckoning a waiter over, he asked whether it would be possible to have a fillet steak. "Oh, yes sir, certainly," came the reply. "And make it very well done," Bill added triumphantly as I sank, utterly defeated, into my chair.

North Warwickshire was another seat fancied by Labour who chose solicitor Mike O'Brien as their candidate. Francis Maude, son of Tory grandee and Thatcher confidante Angus Maude, was defending the seat he surprisingly won in 1983. Both O'Brien and Maude put much time into attempting to get favourable coverage in the *Evening Telegraph*. Maude ran an energetic campaign and invited me several times to meet him on the trail, where he was always surrounded by enthusiastic Young Conservatives in a pub. Both men could be prickly about media reports. O'Brien didn't like me mentioning the fact that he was not from North Warwickshire, while Maude objected to a description of him as having attended a public school. Abingdon School in Oxfordshire was an independent direct grant institution when he was there and only switched to a private fee-paying school later, he insisted.

Maude ran out the winner in North Warwickshire with a majority of 2,829. O'Brien would take the seat five years' later at the 1992 General Election and went on to hold several ministerial positions in the governments of Tony Blair before being defeated in North Warwickshire by Tory Craig Tracey in the 2010 General Election. Maude, meanwhile, was handed a safe Tory seat in Sussex.

Polling day for the 1987 General Election, June 11, was my first experience of the way the *Coventry Telegraph* approached such an event. My reporting team for the night met at the Town Wall for champagne and then went by taxis to the Chase Hotel for a politically-themed dinner where waiters were dressed with party rosettes and the menu included the likes of "Tory turkey" and "Labour liver". The cost of the dinner and cab was covered by the company, and a similarly generous arrangement applied for the 1992 General Election. By the time of the 1997 General Election, alas, the expenses ship had sailed and we had to pay for our own champagne and dinner.

We worked through the night for the 1987 General Election, finishing at about 8am the following day after completing a results round-up for the first edition of the Friday paper. Then onwards to political reporter Len Freeman's house in Earlsdon for 'election cocktails' and breakfast. I left after one drink to get home to my wife and seven-day-old baby son, but the rest of the gang got stuck into the booze and were comatose on sofas and chairs by the time Freeman's father discovered the disarray during a mid-morning visit to the house.

Chapter Thirty

Coventry Council Feels the Squeeze

B y the end of the 1980s councils feeling the effects of the Government's public sector spending squeeze were beginning to make difficult and unpopular decisions about cutting town hall services. Regional newspapers responded by looking more closely than before at local authority waste and profligacy to see where councils might generate more-acceptable savings that could then be diverted to pay for front-line services.

In Coventry the microscope fell on the city council's liking for wining and dining, in particular the spending of the Lord Mayor, Cllr Arthur Waugh Jnr. As Waugh began to reach the end of his year in office in April 1989 the council's finance officers reported that the Lord Mayor's £76,745 hospitality budget was in danger of being overspent. Although the amount set aside for mayoral entertaining was generous – equivalent to £190,000 today – it became clear Waugh simply couldn't keep his spending within budget, and he was forced to cancel three civic dinners before handing over the chains of office in May 1989. Even then, he still overspent on entertaining by £4,000. By contrast, Leicester city council's budget for mayoral entertaining that year stood at just £10,000.

Four years earlier, the *Evening Telegraph* had reported Coventry Labour councillor Richard Morris hitting out at the cost of the mayoralty, in particular the budget for entertaining, describing in colourful language some of his council colleagues as "bestial near-alcoholics", and adding for good measure that the civic office was being used as "a private drinking club for old chums". Ex-councillor Morris was probably referring to the tradition at the end of monthly council meetings for councillors to be invited to the Lord Mayor's parlour for free drinks, sessions that usually went on for a considerable period of time.

Historically, Coventry council had consistently spent more on the civic function than neighbouring authorities, and attempted to justify this by arguing that being a "city of peace and reconciliation" with its bombed-out cathedral a symbol of the futility of war gave it an international status and attracted VIP visitors who had to be treated accordingly. By 1999, Coventry city council was spending £350,000 a year on all aspects of the mayoralty – equivalent to almost £600,000 today after inflation is added.

But the council did not at that time publish details of the cost of individual events hosted by the Lord Mayor. I decided to try to find out exactly what and on whom the Lord Mayor had been spending public money. Finance committee chair Bob Ainsworth promised more openness in future, but four months after Waugh's year in office ended Ainsworth refused to make public a report setting out estimated costs of civic functions for the new Lord Mayor, Cllr David Cairns. Council lawyers helped him out by ruling that a report containing details about the Lord Mayor's functions could not be made public because it was not listed on the finance committee agenda, which was handy for the council and infuriating for me.

In the days before the Freedom of Information Act there was little that the paper could do to force the council to hand over the paperwork, although I hinted to Ainsworth that we might be prepared to seek a judicial review of the decision to deny us the information. This was something I made up on the spur of the moment and I have no idea whether the newspaper would ever have gone to such lengths, probably not, but the suggestion may have had an impact. Under Ainsworth's orders the council relented and handed over a full breakdown of Cllr Waugh's spending on wining and dining during his year in office.

The accounts were fascinating and for the first time Coventry citizens could see exactly what the Lord Mayor had spent taxpayers' money on. Many lunches, dinners and drinks receptions were for trade unions, local Labour parties and sports clubs with which the Lord Mayor was associated, although there was never any suggestion that Waugh acted improperly or did not go through the council's agreed procedures when drawing up guest lists. He was merely doing what his predecessors had done, but made the mistake of drawing attention to himself by failing to stay within budget at a time when local government finances were under greater media scrutiny than ever before.

The adverse publicity certainly didn't inflict much harm on Waugh in the long term. He went on to become deputy leader of the council and was instrumental in calling time on the city's loss-making building services unit – Coventry Contract Services. Waugh telephoned me at home on a Friday in July 1998 asking me to come into the Council House the next day so that he could brief me on a fast-breaking story. The very idea of a council media briefing taking place on a Saturday was unheard of, and Waugh did not disappoint with what he had to say.

As the *Evening Telegraph* reported, a loss-making contract to repair council houses that had been awarded to CCS was put together by Labour politicians and local authority officers at an improperly constituted secret meeting. The decision to tender for the work at an unrealistic price was never approved or discussed either by the management board of CCS or by the full city council. The contract led to a £6 million loss for the public purse, with the result that 14 council employees were suspended and the council was forced to mount an inquiry into the conduct of CCS.

No proper minutes of the meeting to approve the tender were taken and the decision to award the contract was kept from the council leader and deputy leader. John Mutton, who went on to become council leader and Lord Mayor, who was not at the meeting, said notes taken of the discussions were of the type "scribbled on the back of fag packets".

It emerged that the contract could only have turned a profit if the council had been prepared to cut costs by closing several works depots and axing scores of jobs, but that decision was never taken. Instead, council officers were "given guidance" by un-named Labour councillors to keep the depots open.

The CCS affair was one of the first examples of a Labour-run council being publicly exposed for bending the rules in an attempt to see off the private sector by keeping a potentially lucrative building services contract in-house, but the tactic failed when the huge financial losses were made public. Stories began to emerge of a questionable use of public money by CCS, with perhaps the most bizarre discovery being that the council managed to sponsor a CCS employee's stock car racing hobby.

The inquiry probed numerous claims including allegations that some Labour councillors arranged for private work on their own homes to be carried out by CCS employees. The claims were not proven and a 61-page report which blamed the debacle on a combination of poor management, over-powerful trade unions, and a lack of control by council leaders.

Labour councillors, who were spared embarrassment by not being named in the report, were found to have advised council officers to drop the cost-cutting savings that would have been necessary to avoid huge losses on the housing repair contract. As a result, politically sensitive plans to scrap a costly bonus system for employees and to close works depots were not pursued, and from that moment CCS was launched on a suicidal course of huge financial losses. Despite the inquiry, no one was ever held publicly accountable for the losses.

CCS was formed in 1992 as part of a reorganisation that saw the separation of client and contractor under the government's Compulsory Competitive Tendering regime. Asked recently by me for his comments on the financial irregularities, Roxburgh revealed that he had been overruled by the politicians when appointing a suitable person to head-up CCS: "I was not involved in CCS business in 1992 except in the appointment of a Director to the newly formed organisation. There was substantial political pressure to appoint the person then heading Building Services. I insisted on a proper appointment process with national advertising.

"There was little external competition for the post, and after interviews, the elected members of the appointment panel still wanted to appoint 'their' internal candidate. I got the leader's support to not appoint and to re-advertise, which we did. I headhunted and managed to attract applications from two talented, experienced people, one of whom was a woman who subsequently went on to head up a much bigger similar outfit in a large London Borough and who, I thought, would have provided just the dynamic leadership needed by CCS at the time. Members decided to appoint the internal candidate – a bad decision!"

Chapter Thirty-One

The Yanks Are Coming

After the 1987 General Election, the *Coventry Evening Telegraph* was hit by a bombshell when Lord Iliffe sold a controlling interest in his newspapers to the American publisher Ralph Ingersoll, ending almost a century of ownership by the Iliffe family. The first anyone at the *CET* knew about such a momentous event was when news of the sale was broken over the Press Association wires in a snap that mentioned only the *Birmingham Post* and *Birmingham Mail* being disposed of. The *Evening Telegraph* news desk breathed a collective sigh of relief and began assuring reporters that Lord Iliffe would never sell his favourite newspaper, after all was not his flat still in situ upstairs? Was not the Double Diamond still on tap? Almost immediately, the PA updated its story to make it clear that all Iliffe's newspapers were to be sold, including the *Coventry Evening Telegraph*. Collapse of severely embarrassed news desk.

Most people on the editorial floor immediately decamped to the Town Wall Tavern to discuss what this might mean for the paper's future. Journalists are natural doom-mongers and most were adamant that Ingersoll must have bought the *Telegraph* to asset strip it and close it down, and the more beer that was consumed the worse the predictions of disaster became. It seemed highly unlikely to me that Ingersoll would wish to close the paper, for why would someone pay a large sum of money for a highly profitable newspaper only to get rid of it?

Ingersoll didn't close the *Telegraph*, but neither did he invest much in quality journalism. A comment reportedly made by one of Ingersoll's executives soon after the sale had been concluded, dismissively describing the "non-advertising content" of the paper as "news holes", served only to underline a general feeling that the *Evening Telegraph*'s hard-earned reputation for brilliant writing was in danger of disappearing pretty quickly.

It soon became clear that the Americans hadn't given much thought to what they wanted to do with their new acquisitions, other than to recoup the cost of their investment by cutting costs and increasing profits, and it remains a mystery to this day why a US publisher with no experience of the British media would want to buy a stable of long-established Midland titles.

One thing that the new American owners did do immediately was to call time on the *CET*'s generous expenses regime. There would be no expenses paid in future without receipts, so journalists couldn't simply claim the odd fiver for 'entertaining contacts' in the pub without proof of a purchase, a change which really only brought us into line with other newspapers at the time. All first class train travel was banned and the subsidised golf society disappeared as eventually did the 21 Club for long-serving members of staff and the canteen and social club, as well as the Christmas bonus and the *Evening Telegraph Yearbook*. The 21 Club made a brief comeback, but then disappeared for good. One by one the perks that made the *CET* such a great and unique place to work were being dismantled as the paper's owners eradicated 'unnecessary' costs in a dash to generate a quick return on their investment.

At the end of 1989 I took on another responsibility in addition to my political editor duties, putting together the *Evening Telegraph*'s first finance page aimed at 'ordinary' people. Family Finance sought to explain in plain language the principles behind pensions, investing in shares and banking. In 1990 the page won the regional finance paper of the year award in a competition run by the Bradford and Bingley building society. My prize was a case of Moet & Chandon and a trip to the Savoy Hotel in London to pick up a plaque, with an overnight stay paid for by the *CET*, although not, sadly, at the Savoy.

Geoff Elliott departed in 1990 to edit the *Portsmouth News*. He took me out to dinner while I was at the Conservative conference in Bournemouth and asked me to join him at Portsmouth as political editor, offering a pay rise to entice me. But the housing market had entered a slump, I was still happy in Coventry, and my wife's parents lived near to us, so I decided it would be unwise to move and declined the offer. As much as I would have liked to work with Geoff again, it's not a decision I ever regretted.

Geoff Elliott was briefly replaced in the editor's chair at Coventry by Ingersoll's UK editorial director Chazy Dowaliby, an American who it soon became apparent was simply minding the shop until a permanent replacement could be found. She will be mostly remembered for keeping a large tin of sweets on her desk which she distributed generously and she also deserves a special mention in this book as the only one of the 15 editors I worked for over 36 years who I felt obliged to politely refuse when asked to write a leader. The subject was a craze among young people for mutant ninja turtle pizzas, a subject about which I knew nothing and cared about even less.

Dowaliby departed Coventry in under a year to be replaced as editor by Neil Benson, a Yorkshireman with an eye to climbing the greasy ladder of management, which he did by becoming editorial director of Trinity Mirror's regional newspapers. Benson was in many ways ahead of his time and instituted consumer journalism with news features on shopping and wanted the paper to take a more up to date view of women and families. Neil was extremely kind to me when I was off work for six weeks with stress and depression and went out of his way to make sure I was looked after upon returning to the office.

Ingersoll's ownership of the newspapers lasted four years before a management buyout led by *Birmingham Post* MD Chris Oakley in 1991 created Midland Independent Newspapers.

Chapter Thirty-Two

Arms to Iraq

During 1992 I was lucky enough to have a ringside seat for one of the most important post-war investigations into Government murkiness, the Scott inquiry into the Arms-to-Iraq affair. The inquiry under Lord Justice Scott was set up following the collapse of a trial into claims that three senior executives of the Coventry firm Matrix Churchill were unlawfully exporting machine tools, which could be used for making military equipment, to Iraq. They were said to have deceived the Government as to the use of the tools when applying for export licences.

They defended themselves on the basis that the Government knew exactly what Matrix Churchill was up to: not least because its managing director, Paul Henderson, had been supplying information about Iraq to the British intelligence agencies on a regular basis.

The judge at the trial overturned Public Interest Immunity Certificates signed by several Ministers that would have enabled key evidence to be withheld from the court, something that probably would have led to the conviction and imprisonment of Henderson and his colleagues. Confidential documents had therefore to be handed over, enabling the defence to show that the export licences were properly granted and that the Matrix Churchill executives were not guilty.

The trial collapsed after Tory MP Alan Clark, who was minister for defence procurement when the export licences were granted, admitted under cross-examination that notes of one meeting at the Department for Trade and Industry were 'economical with the actualité' and he knew full well the machine tools could be used to manufacture munitions.

Severely embarrassed by the fact that the Government had seemingly conspired to export machinery for making lethal weapons to the Iraqi dictator Saddam Hussein, prime minister John Major was forced into conceding a public inquiry to get to the bottom of the incident.

The Inquiry was set up on a non-statutory basis and was tasked with examining defence and dual-use exports to Iraq, whether Ministers stuck to Government policy, and the use of the Public Interest Immunity Certificates.

Lord Justice Scott's hearings took place at Buckingham Gate in London, close to Buckingham Palace and St James's Park. It is doubtful today given the cost of travelling and subsistence whether a regional newspaper would staff such an inquiry, even one with local implications, but I was sent to almost every sitting of the Scott inquiry and heard evidence from star witnesses including Margaret Thatcher, John Major, Michael Heseltine, Kenneth Clarke, Lord Howe, Douglas Hurd and Alan Clark, as well as Sir Robin Butler, the cabinet secretary.

It is generally accepted that the Scott Report represents the most exhaustive study produced of the individual responsibility of ministers to Parliament. Scott comments on the difficulty of extracting from departments the required documents (some 130,000 of them in all) and notes how Customs and Excise could not find out what Ministry of Defence export policy was, and how intelligence reports were not passed on to those who needed to know.

The *Economist* commented that "Sir Richard exposed an excessively secretive government machine, riddled with incompetence, slippery with the truth and willing to mislead Parliament". The report struck at the heart of Whitehall secrecy and characterised the nature of the government:

"The main objectives of governments are the implementation of their policies and the discomfiture of opposition; they do not submit with enthusiasm to the restraints of accountability ... governments are little disposed to volunteer information that may expose them to criticism ... The enforcement of accountability depends largely on the ability of Parliament to prise information from governments which are inclined to be defensively secretive where they are most vulnerable to challenge."

Scott eventually published his report in 1996 and the findings undoubtedly added to the general national mood of anger with John Major's government which by now was in freefall and heading towards certain disaster at the 1997 General Election.

Scott identified three main areas of concern. First, the Import, Export and Customs Powers (Defence) Act 1939 was emergency legislation passed at the outbreak of the Second World War which allowed the government to issue regulations which were not subject to resolutions in Parliament, for the duration of the emergency, which would make it a criminal offence to export certain goods to named countries. While the Act should have been lapsed at the end of the war in 1945, it remained in force.

The second area was the failure of ministerial accountability; the principle that "for every action of a servant of the crown a minister is answerable to Parliament".

The third area was that of public interest certificates, the so-called gagging orders, which had been issued during the Matrix Churchill trial. Scott concluded that, as a result of these certificates, innocent men were in danger of being sent to prison, because the government would not allow the defence counsel to see the documents that would exonerate their clients. While some of these contained potentially sensitive intelligence material, many were simply internal communications: the certificates were intended to protect the ministers and civil servants who had written the communications, rather than the public interest.

The report had to be debated in Parliament. Ministers criticised were given advanced access to Scott's findings and briefed extensively on how to defend themselves against the key criticisms. In contrast, the opposition were given just two hours to read the million-plus words. John Major decided that a vote against the Government would be in effect a vote of no confidence and trigger a General Election, ensuring that Conservative MPs would not vote against, while a vote for was a vote exonerating the Government of any wrongdoing. I was in the Commons press gallery that night to witness a stunning performance by Shadow Foreign Secretary Robin Cook, who worked through the Scott Report with surgical brilliance. Nonetheless, the Government won the vote 320–319 and was able to limp on until being put out of its misery at a General Election the following year.

Anger over the case in Coventry was confined chiefly to Matrix Churchill's collapse as a going concern after Paul Henderson and his fellow directors were arrested, throwing hundreds of people out of work. What tended to be overlooked at the time was the inconvenient fact that Matrix Churchill had for several years been wholly owned by Saddam Hussein's Iraqi government and was therefore never likely to be the source of stable long-term employment that many people fondly imagined.

In the run-up to the 1997 General Election Labour MPs, displaying breath-taking political opportunism, campaigned for former Matrix Churchill workers to be financially compensated by the Tory Government. Once in office, however, the new Labour government showed a distinct disinterest in paying anything to the former workforce. The compensation campaign continued in Coventry until 2001, backed by unions but, significantly, no longer by Labour MPs. The Matrix Churchill victims never received a penny, even from a Labour government.

Chapter Thirty-Three

New MPs and New Editors

T he 1992 General Election saw two new Coventry Labour MPs burst on to the scene – Jim Cunningham took Coventry South-west from John Butcher, while Bob Ainsworth won the safe seat of Coventry North-east replacing left-winger John Hughes who had been deselected by the constituency Labour party. Cunningham was the leader of Coventry City Council at the time and Ainsworth was his deputy. Both were deemed to be on the centre-right of the party.

Hughes was a former Coventry city councillor, and chair of the Coventry District Labour Party from 1977 to 1981. While on the council he was expelled three times from the ruling Labour group for defying the party whip over spending cuts, rent rises and school meal price rises. In the mid-1980s, with the hard-left in the ascendency, Hughes was selected to replace sitting MP George Park as Labour candidate for Coventry North-east at the 1987 General Election thereby inheriting one of the party's safest seats in the country. By 1992, with Militant and the hard-left under attack, Ainsworth seized his chance. The deselection of John Hughes and the selection of Ainsworth was a grubby affair with claims from Hughes' supporters that some Labour members long since dead and others who were out of the country at the time had somehow managed to vote in the selection process, and that a large number of postal vote forms were filled out in the same handwriting. There was nothing particularly confined to Coventry about allegations of voting fraud among Asian communities in inner city areas. Similar claims about postal vote irregularities were to crop up from time to time across the country as the Labour party continued with its eternal struggle of left versus right.

I'd formed a good relationship with Bob since his time as chair of the city council finance committee. He was very wary at first of talking to a journalist, taking the view shared by many of his colleagues that the *Coventry Evening Telegraph* was the Labour-bashing enemy and not to be trusted. But we shared a similar background – brought up in poor working-class households with a determination to get on in life – and we both took a pragmatic view of politics.

Bob had been a fitter at Jaguar's Browns Lane plant in Coventry after leaving school and progressed up through the trade union movement, starting off as a young shop steward when none of his fellow workmates wanted the job, and becoming branch president of the Manufacturing, Science and Finance union before being elected to the city council in 1984. A week after he became the MP for Coventry North-east I was a guest of Bob and his wife Gloria at lunch in the House of Commons. I told Bob his life had changed for ever, financially and professionally, and no one was more delighted than me when he became deputy chief whip, Armed Forces Minister, a Privy Counsellor, and finally in 2010 Secretary of State for Defence.

His appointment to the cabinet by prime minister Gordon Brown underlined Ainsworth's toughness. Media speculation that the defence job would go to Labour MP Shaun Woodward was rife, and with very good reason for government sources made it known to Ainsworth that Woodward, a multi-millionaire former Tory MP reputed to have a butler in his mansion, who joined Labour under Tony Blair, was within a whisker of being handed the defence portfolio. Ainsworth, bravely and to his eternal credit, made sure that Brown got the following message: "If you appoint the Tory, you'll be looking for a new Armed Forces Minister because I'll not work with him." Brown backed down and made Ainsworth Defence Secretary, although the appointment was confirmed by telephone. The prime minister apparently didn't have the time to meet in person his new cabinet member.

Neil Benson remained in Coventry for only two years and was replaced as editor by Dan Mason, the deputy editor of the *Birmingham Mail*. Mason was about as far removed from the traditional regional newspaper editor as can be imagined. A dapper man and sharp dresser with a penchant for wearing bow ties and a keen interest in the arts, he was an accomplished drummer and once gave a performance at a party held to celebrate the *Telegraph* winning an award for the biggest increase in circulation of any regional newspaper (those were the days). With his dark hair swept back and sporting a 'mullet' as favoured by professional footballers in the 1970s, Mason earned the nickname in the newsroom of Lionel Blair after the television personality to whom he bore a passing resemblance.

Mason had only been in the chair for a few weeks when I turned up a story of some embarrassment for the police. It concerned a maverick Warwickshire Tory county councillor, John Findon, who was chair of the council police committee. Findon, an outspoken man who didn't mind who he upset, let it be known to friends that he was opposed to wearing a seat belt in a car and would ignore the change in law making the wearing of belts compulsory. His 'friends' passed this information onto me and I rang Findon, hardly expecting him to admit refusing to wear a seat belt, but he did so and embellished the story by claiming there were plenty of examples of drivers being killed in crashes because they couldn't release their seat belts and were as a consequence trapped and burnt to death in their wrecked vehicles.

Mason came over to my desk to ask somewhat nervously whether I was sure I'd got the story right. I assured him I had spoken to Findon and the story was correct. We splashed on Findon in our county editions, but that wasn't the end of the controversial councillor. A year or so later he found himself at Oxford Crown Court accused of assaulting a police officer. Findon pleaded not guilty, claiming that a 'punch' was simply a friendly tap in the stomach. His trump card was to produce as a character witness Peter Joslin the chief constable of Warwickshire. Findon was cleared of any wrongdoing.

Dan Mason had an interest in politics, but was not as open about his background with me as perhaps he ought to have been. After he had been in post for a few months Labour party sources tipped me off that members of Mason's very close family were active Conservatives in Leicestershire. I certainly wasn't aware of the connection. This did not mean of course that Dan Mason was a Conservative or even if he was that he used his newspaper to promote the Tory cause and to bash Labour, in fact I found him to be scrupulously even-handed and happy to bash all political parties if a robust case for doing so could be made. But in a place like Coventry even the merest link with the Conservative party was enough to send Labour city councillors and MPs into a frenzy and as far as they were concerned Mason's arrival was further proof that the *Evening Telegraph* was a Tory rag.

Chapter Thirty-Four

1997 General Election

A s the 1997 General Election approached it became obvious from huge opinion poll leads that Tony Blair's 'New Labour' was on course to win a resounding victory and bring 18 years of Tory rule to an end. John Major was looking increasingly beleaguered as prime minister and did not appear to be receiving the best media advice from his inner circle.

Major visited the Jaguar Cars plant at Browns Lane in Coventry a couple of months before the election where, most embarrassingly from the company's point of view, he was booed by a handful of workers as he toured the factory. The visit was notable for an inexplicable decision that Major would give no interviews to local newspapers. It was explained that Tory HQ had decided "today will be a national broadcast media day". If he'd set out deliberately to visit Coventry with the express intention of annoying the local media, he couldn't have caused a self-inflicted wound any more effectively. Tony Blair toured the same factory during the campaign, but made certain to give a brief interview to every local newspaper reporter present, albeit with a brooding Alistair Campbell sat in the corner of the room to keep an eye on his master's voice as I quizzed Blair about Labour's plans for taxes.

As if to make amends, or more likely out of sheer desperation given the dreadful headlines the government was attracting in the national media, I was invited to Downing Street to interview Major a few weeks before the 1997 General Election campaign began. Major in the flesh was exactly as his image would have it – a nice man, but rather dull and grey with nothing very imaginative or newsworthy to say. He ushered me into the cabinet room at Number 10 with the words: "Good morning Mr Dale. Did you come down from Coventry on the train? Was it on time?" I did, and it was, as it happened.

As I took out a pen and notebook to get down to business the prime minister motioned towards the end of the room where I'd failed to notice a man wearing a huge set of headphones sat hunched over an extremely old-fashioned recording device with large reels of tape. Major said: "There's no need to write anything down Mr Dale, we record everything in here and you can have a full transcript in a couple of hours." I'd assumed, of course, that our conversation would be recorded, but I'd imagined something rather more sophisticated at the heart of the British government than a spook in the corner of the room operating a tape recorder that appeared to be a relic from the 1950s

The only thing of any note that Major had to say was an admission that the Conservative Party would never be able to persuade voters it was serious about investing in the National Health Service. There would have to be radical changes to the way the NHS worked to meet growing demand from increasing longevity, but only the Labour Party would be able to get away with change because voters would always be suspicious about any Tory plan to reform the health service. Paradoxically though, Labour would never impose any substantial changes to the way the NHS went about its business because the party remained emotionally wedded to how the health service had always operated since 1947. It was a wholly correct but rather depressing analysis, I thought.

Major gave me about 30 minutes of his time, which was extremely gracious of him, and unlike many politicians did not avoid tough questions and attempted to answer everything I asked. But I can't imagine he would have been overjoyed with the finished product if he ever saw it, an *Evening Telegraph* double-page spread with a huge heading reproducing one of my blunter questions: "Prime Minister, are you the only person in the country who thinks you can win the next election?"

The approaching election saw attention focused on Geoffrey Robinson as the national media began to pick up on the Coventry MP's close links with Gordon Brown and Tony Blair and there was intense speculation as to the role he might play in a Labour government. It was assumed Robinson would get a top job which he did, serving as Paymaster General from May 1997 until he was forced to resign in December 1998 after it was revealed he had lent New Labour guru Peter Mandelson £373,000 to buy a house, and the payment had not been declared. Robinson had already seen off criticism a year earlier when it became known that he was the beneficiary of a £13 million trust fund based in the Channel Islands. There was nothing remotely illegal or improper about that, but Geoffrey's wealth and personal financial arrangements were not to the liking of Labour's hard left.

I had a sneaking admiration for Robinson, a charismatic far from run of the mill politician who became managing director of Jaguar Cars at a ridiculously young age and went on to make a fortune as a businessman. He first won Coventry North-west at a by-election in 1976, helped by a clever media campaign projecting the successful businessman as just one of the lads – a famous picture showed a shirt-sleeved Robinson surrounded by track workers tucking into sausage and chips in the Jaguar canteen. He'd even learnt a trick from the H P Sauce-loving prime minister Harold Wilson, with a bottle placed next to his plate. What could have been more egalitarian than a gaffer who eats with the lads and likes a shake of Birmingham's finest condiment on his plate? That, at least, was the impression given, although in reality Robinson was more at home in expensive French restaurants than workplace canteens.

Chauffeur-driven in a top of the range Jaguar, Robinson inevitably attracted criticism from hair-shirt Labour members who took an instant dislike to his champagne lifestyle and stunning property portfolio – an Edwin Lutyens mansion in Surrey as well as homes in Tuscany and the south of France, and a second Lutyens mansion that he restored and sold. But Robinson did not inherit his wealth. He took a personal gamble in founding technology company TransTec which paid off and made him a very rich man.

I was asked to grab a few words with Robinson on the night he resigned from the government. He cut a sad figure getting off the train at Coventry, alone with a bag slung over his shoulder having cleared his desk a couple of hours before and he didn't have much to add to his resignation statement. But we had an evocative picture of a despondent Robinson in the foggy gloom of a cold December evening.

Robinson almost didn't make it into the Government at all. He was lucky to survive a deselection attempt by the hard-left before the 1992 General Election, narrowly beating off a challenge by Coventry teacher Will Reese. When the votes at the Coventry North-west constituency party selection meeting were counted, Robinson edged home by less than one percent. The left's campaign was based partly on the MP's refusal to live in his constituency, or even to do what many other members of parliament do and buy a token house for occasional overnight stops. Instead, Robinson stopped at the four-star Holiday Inn hotel at Allesley, on the western edge of the city, whenever he was in Coventry, much to the disgust of Militant.

After the re-selection scare West Midlands Labour Party decided that Robinson required more favourable media coverage in Coventry. He had become one of *Peeping Tom*'s regular victims, with an endless barrage of stories focusing on his wealth and champagne socialist lifestyle. Labour decided to appoint a young press officer to represent the MP in the shape of

Ian Austin, a former teacher from Walsall, who in 1999 became political adviser to Gordon Brown and was elected MP for Dudley North. I can't recall Austin making much of a difference to the mixed media coverage that inevitably came Robinson's way. He must have discovered fairly quickly that Geoffrey Robinson is not the type of person who can be told what to say, or what not to say, by a press minder.

In the run-up to the 1997 election Robinson was busy doing Gordon Brown's bidding by making the case for Britain joining the single European currency, the euro. At that time Brown was leaning towards supporting British entry, although he quickly swung full circle and changed his mind on becoming Chancellor by publishing five tests that would have to be met if we were to join the single currency. It was immediately clear the tests had been designed in such a way that they could never be met, and Britain was thus permitted by Brussels not to join the euro.

Robinson invited me and the *Evening Telegraph*'s news editor Peter Mitchell to join him for lunch, at Lino's of course, to discuss the forthcoming election. We arrived at the appointed hour but there was no sign of Geoffrey. After a while a clearly agitated Lino came across to explain Signor Robinson had telephoned to say he was running a little late but had asked whether we would have drinks, anything we wanted, and put them on his bill? Is the Pope a Catholic? Several large gin and tonics were downed in rapid fashion before Lino reappeared, in a state of even greater consternation.

Signor Robinson was holding on the phone and wished to speak to one of us. Mitchell took the call and it became clear that Geoffrey, who was driving himself for some unfathomable reason, hadn't a clue how to find Lino's even though he must have been taken to the restaurant countless times. In the days before satellite navigation, Mitchell had to talk the MP to Lino's, where he eventually arrived full of apologies for keeping us waiting. As if by magic, after a long and boozy lunch, we emerged from the restaurant to discover that Geoffrey's chauffeur had arrived in a second Jaguar to take the MP home, which was probably just as well. No one knew what happened to the first Jaguar, but presumably one of Geoffrey's staff was despatched to drive it home.

At the Labour conference in Blackpool in 1996, Geoffrey kindly extended a lunch invitation, picking me up in the Jaguar to go to the Seafood Restaurant near the South Pier. The building didn't look very promising from the outside, but the menu seemed decent enough and we were the only customers. After a couple of gin and tonics, Geoffrey called for the wine list. "There is only one thing worth drinking here," he announced to a startled waitress, "and that is the Bollinger." So, we had a bottle of champagne. After consulting a menu we decided that lobster would be rather good. "Would that be half a lobster each, sir?", the waitress asked tentatively. Geoffrey scoffed: "Good grief, no. Whole lobsters, please." The conversation rattled around the next General Election and Labour's chances of forming a Government, which were clearly excellent. We touched on the euro, which Geoffrey was very keen on the UK joining at the time. Then the champagne ran out, so we had another bottle of Bollinger. Not a lot of work was done by me that afternoon, obviously, although I can't speak for Geoffrey.

The days following Tony Blair's election victory in 1997 were marked in the political world by a feeling that 'new Labour' was going to be a very different, modern kind of government, open and inclusive. The bold promise was quickly dashed, of course, but the change in Downing Street did initially deliver a welcome new approach to regional newspapers by the government. During the first couple of weeks of the Blair administration the *Coventry Evening Telegraph* and other Midland publications received an invitation to meet the new Home Secretary, Jack Straw, for an informal briefing session. Unusually, Straw made it clear he wanted to meet reporters who would actually be writing about the government, rather than editors and managers.

I made my way to the Belfry Hotel, near Birmingham, where the Home Office had hired a room and put on lunch for Straw and invited journalists. The Home Secretary was charm personified and happy to discuss a wide range of subjects around his portfolio. Nothing was off limits – crime, prison policy, terrorism – and we left believing the meeting heralded a new approach by one of Blair's closest lieutenants to dealing with the media. Straw's farewell promise was along the lines that 'we must do this again' and that such get-togethers would be regular occurrences. Predictably enough the government's honeymoon period soon ended and we never received an invitation for another cosy chat with the Home Secretary.

Chapter Thirty-Five

CET's Love-in with the Council

D an Mason's editorship between 1993 and 1998 signalled an escalation of the community-based approach by the *CET* which began under Neil Benson, although this would often be at the expense of 'hard news' stories. Mason wanted news to be positive if at all possible. He wanted the paper to get on with Coventry council and to champion the city's attempts at economic and cultural regeneration, even refusing to appoint a crime reporter, claiming that readers were fed up with murder and mayhem all over the front page, although no evidence for this assumption was ever forthcoming.

Mason's approach was no doubt music to the ears of Coventry council chief executive Iain Roxburgh, who had been in-post since 1988 and had felt the full sting of hostile media coverage over the Coventry Contract Services saga. Roxburgh, who drove up from London for his interview on a 1,100cc BMW motorbike, was inevitably dubbed 'Rocky Roxburgh' by *Peeping Tom*. When his appointment was announced I immediately recognised the name. Roxburgh was the Labour party candidate for my home constituency of Henley-on-Thames at the 1983 General Election where he came a distant third behind Michael Heseltine for the Tories and the Liberal candidate. He had also been a Labour councillor in the London borough of Brent.

The *CET*'s new love-in with Coventry did not always go according to plan. On one occasion Mason asked reporters to contact famous Coventrians and obtain from them a testimonial for what makes their city great which would then be splashed across a special *Telegraph* promotional article. One famous television personality at the time, who hailed from Coventry, who shall remain nameless, was telephoned and asked to comment on the attractions of his home town. His reply was less than helpful: "Coventry's a shit-hole. Always has been, always will be."

In February 1998 we published an eight-page supplement eulogising the city council's regeneration plans for the decade to come, which were said to amount to £700 million of new build, under the gushing headline: "It's simply breathtaking." The supplement, written largely by me, was pure hype and must have pleased everyone in the Council House no end, although no one at the local authority had the good grace to say thanks for what amounted to thousands of pounds of free advertising. Dan wrote to me afterwards: "Thank you for your magnificent efforts in putting together the breathtaking Coventry supplement. It struck exactly the balance I had hoped for, being both positive yet realistic."

I had mixed feelings about this approach. While I was more than happy to promote the council's successes such as they were, in particular in improving the city centre, Mason's determination to forge a closer relationship made it difficult when it fell to me to expose the local authority's shortcomings, which were still plentiful. Council leaders, as ever, seemed only to notice the critical stories and were either oblivious to our efforts to champion Coventry, or if they did recognise the paper's fresh approach they didn't say so publicly.

A flashpoint concerned the plans of Coventry City FC, then still in the Premier League of English football, to move from its cramped Highfield Road city centre ground to a new purpose-built stadium on land near Holbrooks in the north-west of the city – the ground opened in 2005 and became known as the Ricoh Arena after Jaguar Cars pulled out of a sponsorship deal. I was the first journalist to reveal the stadium proposal, much to the anger of Coventry City who feared publicity might sabotage the club's highly secret talks about the move with the city council and with Tesco who would pay £66.5 million for 30 acres of land next to the stadium for a new superstore.

The club implored Mason to stop me writing about the scheme until they were ready to go public. But Mason, to his credit, agreed to publish my story.

Coventry City did eventually move to the Ricoh but the club's stay was unhappy. It quickly emerged that the club did not actually own the new ground, something that led to years of fierce rows with the council. The stadium was initially operated by Arena Coventry Limited (ACL), with Coventry City as tenants. ACL was owned jointly by Coventry city council and the Alan Edward Higgs Charity. Following a protracted rent dispute between Coventry City and ACL, the football club left the Ricoh Arena in 2013, playing home matches at in Northampton for over a year before returning to the Ricoh in September 2014. Within two months, both shareholders in ACL were bought out by rugby union club Wasps, who relocated to the stadium from their previous ground. Relations between Coventry City FC and Wasps broke down again and the football club is now playing its 'home' matches in Birmingham.

Chapter Thirty-Six

Perks of the Job

U nfortunately, poor rates of pay for regional journalists go with the territory. During 36 years on newspapers the peak of my earnings ability was £34,000 a year in 2011 on *The Birmingham Post*. Partly this is a matter of supply and demand since there will always be far more people wishing to become a journalist than there will be jobs available. In fact, so desperate are graduates to get a toehold in the media that newspapers, radio and television stations routinely offer a month or two of 'work experience' at either no pay or very little pay and there is never any shortage of takers for such arrangements. Only in recent years have work experience recruits been permitted to write articles for publication. Editors would not have considered for a moment letting loose unqualified journalists on their newspapers twenty or thirty years ago and the National Union of Journalists would have had something to say too, but staffing cuts and depleted newsrooms have meant that most publications are prepared now to take the risk of having unqualified 'journalists' on board.

It's also the case that the attention of newspaper management is generally focused on advertising, which is regarded as the money-making department. Ingersoll, the *Coventry Evening Telegraph*'s American owners, were fond of dismissing news stories as 'the filling around the advertising' and saw no need at all to invest in quality journalism. They also took the view that annual pay rises had to be earned through improved productivity, much to the horror of most of my colleagues who liked to argue that a reporter's worth could not be measured solely by the number of words written. Some major investigative pieces might take months to put together with little to show in terms of output for the reporters involved, or might not even make it into the paper at all.

There are of course many ways in which regional journalists have always managed to improve their finances, with selling news stories to national newspapers an obvious example. I once sold a 250-word piece about a Coventry MP to the *Mail on Sunday*'s gossip column for a payment that was roughly equivalent to my weekly wage at the *CET*. Journalists wishing to cultivate national newspapers could improve their bank balances substantially, although I never had the time or inclination to undertake more than the odd flurry into the world of freelance journalism.

Of far more interest was the world of the newspaper 'freebie' such as free holidays, for which demand in the news room was understandably intense. The deal was simple: travel companies would give a journalist a free holiday in return for a newspaper review of said holiday. The most prized travel breaks included free places for your partner and children, thereby providing an annual family holiday for free.

It was never explicitly spelt out that the review ought to be favourable, but anyone wishing to qualify for further holidays would have been mad to file a critical piece. In any case, most of the holidays on offer were high-end breaks with luxury accommodation which the travel companies had an interest in promoting and hard-up journalists would never otherwise have been able to afford.

A question arose: how could these holidays be divided up fairly to make sure everyone who wanted a free break would be given at least one per year? It was a question that lurked in the background but was never really faced up to, let alone answered. Ultimately, holidays were used by news desks and features editors to reward favoured reporters, and the higher up the pecking order you were the more exotic the holiday likely to come your way. Editors, deputy editors, news editors and features editors would get the luxury cruises and trips to America. The highest regarded reporters would be handed trips to the Mediterranean. Junior staff might be given a boating holiday on the Norfolk Broads or a weekend break in Blackpool if they were lucky.

I openly admit to enjoying more than my fair share of free trips over the years, most of them while I was at the *Coventry Telegraph*. In the early 1990s press trips to France were readily available and left some fantastic memories. Once I took part in a rally across the Burgundy region where journalists from regional newspapers drove hired cars from expensive hotel to expensive hotel, gorging and drinking ourselves stupid each night. On another occasion I stayed at the La Assiette Champenoise hotel in Reims with its three-star Michelin restaurant where we sampled what our host described as "in my view the five best champagne vintages of the 20th century". In the Vosges we went on an early morning trip into the mountains to spot chamois. Breakfast was laid on at a remote inn where mine-host insisted we tried his home-made chestnut liqueur which tasted appalling and resembled rocket fuel. As it was nine in the morning I took care to jettison most of my drink into a flower pot when no one was looking. But the kindly inn-keeper, assuming I'd bolted mine down, insisted on refilling my glass to the top and watched approvingly while I drank it.

For about six or seven years I benefited from skiing press trips courtesy visiting many of the top European resorts including Wengen, Klosters, Kitzbuhel, Alpe du Huez, Passo Tonale and Zell am Zee. My hosts generously provided free meals, hire of skis and lessons. This was of course a tremendous perk and something I could never have afforded on the *Evening Telegraph*'s wages. My part of the bargain was to provide 700-word articles for the paper's travel section, which was hardly an onerous task.

For about a year I was the *Evening Telegraph*'s restaurant critic, dining out once a week for free across Coventry and Warwickshire, usually accompanied by my wife and sometimes by friends. Naturally, no one believes me when I say that the business of critiquing a restaurant every week becomes a bit of a chore after a while. The process of having to take secretive notes makes it difficult to relax and a social occasion becomes just another job albeit an enjoyable one. As might have been expected, I generally chose the best and most expensive eating spots, prompting Dave Nellist to write a letter to the *Evening Telegraph* complaining that I spent more on one meal than many people in Coventry have to live on in a week. The MP's claim was an exaggeration, but only just. The *Telegraph*'s American owners baulked at the cost, and it was suggested to me that I concentrate on cheap pub food instead. I declined, and my days as a restaurant critic ended abruptly.

Chapter Thirty-Seven

Coombe Abbey and Baginton

As local government spending cuts began to bite in the early 1990s, Coventry council in common with most other local authorities started to consider making money by selling property assets. The leasing of Coombe Abbey to the No Ordinary Hotels Group provoked a public outburst stirred up by Militant, and certainly tested Dan Mason's wish that we find 'good news stories' to write about the council. The council had allowed the Grade I listed building, parts of which date back to the 13th century, to dilapidate to such an extent that millions of pounds in repairs would have been needed to keep the popular attraction open to the public. But the decision to turn Coombe Abbey into a four-star hotel obviously raised a huge question as to whether councils ought to be in the business of owning hotels.

Militant exploited the 'selling the family jewels' line and claimed that ordinary Coventrians would be priced out of enjoying the park and would never be able to afford to use what was to become a luxury hotel. Militant didn't explain where the council could get the money from to repair Coombe Abbey, but their concern about affordability was quickly proven when free parking for people wishing to visit Coombe park disappeared and hefty charges were imposed by the new owners.

Ironically, in 2017 the council bought back for an undisclosed sum the Coombe Abbey lease it had sold 20 years earlier, claiming the hotel was an asset that would generate revenue for the public purse for years to come, quoting an estimated ten percent annual return.

On the subject of businesses that local authorities do not generally own, Coventry Airport at Baginton on the south-west border of the city was for many years the council's major property asset and proved to be an expensive and contentious luxury. In 1994 Labour councillors were angered to discover flights out of the airport operated by Phoenix Aviation, a company owned by Rugby businessman Christopher Barrett-Jolley, were exporting live calves destined to become veal to France and Holland. Their anger may have been understandable, but Barrett-Jolley had the weight of the law on his side as he was not acting unlawfully and had been given permission to undertake the flights by the airport's managers.

On December 21 1994 an Air Algerie Boeing 737 leased to Phoenix Aviation crashed on returning from a veal trip to Amsterdam with the loss of the crew of five. The death toll would have been far higher had the pilot not heroically managed to avoid a nearby housing estate.

The airport became the target for protest demonstrations with regular battles erupting between animal rights activists and the police. Tragically, in February 1995, Jill Phipps, a protester aged 31, was crushed to death under the wheels of a lorry carrying live calves into the airport as police tried to clear a way in for the vehicle.

Global publicity arising out of Phipps's death prompted Phoenix voluntarily to suspend operations until January 26 1995 when flights to Amsterdam resumed.

The council was desperate for an end to the veal flights, and so were the police who clearly didn't want the expense and the hassle of guaranteeing safe passage for trucks carrying the calves into the airport. It quickly became clear the police were unwilling to uphold their duty to make sure people could go about their lawful business, even if that business was repugnant to a very small minority.

Warwickshire's assistant chief constable wrote to the council:

"Should the flights re-start I would anticipate the return of demonstrators, probably in greater numbers than we have previously experienced. My clear responsibility is to ensure the free passage of the vehicles into your airport, whilst at the same time accommodating protest within the law. My concerns at this time, however, relate not to that aspect of the situation, but the possible outcome of a police operation which, if successful, allows vehicles to gain entry to the airport. In fact, I have very grave concerns for the integrity of airside safety and security should vehicles carrying animals actually gain access."

He explained that his concerns were based upon intelligence reports, incidents which had already occurred within the perimeter of the airport, a recognition that the underlying issue of animal welfare was causing "an intensity of emotion ... leading many reasonable people to behave in a direct and confrontational way", the ineffectiveness of the existing perimeter fence, the virtual total absence of security staff, and his recognition that "incursion by even a few demonstrator ... would ... seriously compromise both ground and air safety conditions".

The letter continued:

"Despite my acknowledged responsibilities in relation to the free passage of vehicles arriving at the airport and the effective management of any protests by demonstrators, the constabulary does not have a responsibility to protect the security of the airport from trespass. In the circumstances I must ask you to undertake, as a matter of urgency, a comprehensive review of your security arrangements and to take whatever steps are necessary to enhance them accordingly."

The content of the police letter, along with implications of a huge bill to provide improved security fencing at the airport, was enough to persuade the council to suspend any further veal flights.

But the decision was challenged by Phoenix Aviation at a judicial review where the High Court ruled that Coventry City Council was wrong to stop the "perfectly legal" flights and had given in to "unlawful threats" by protesters and had given no consideration "to the awesome implications for the rule of law" by banning a lawful activity. A lawful trade in live animals was not to be interrupted for fear of public disorder, the court found.

Following Jill Phipps's death, Barrett-Jolley's home was besieged and attacked by protesters and he was arrested after allegedly firing an air rifle at them. Continuing protests over the veal flights prompted Barrett-Jolley to hire John Bradshaw, a Warwickshire-based public relations specialist, in an attempt to counter the constant stream of negative publicity about Phoenix Aviation's veal flights in the *Evening Telegraph* as well as national newspapers and television news.

Bradshaw had his work cut out, and as he began to undertake the task of being Barrett-Jolley's press spokesman found himself the subject of several death threats from animal rights activists based in Brighton. He took an accurate but uncompromising line with the media – that Barrett-Jolley was acting within the law, that Coventry council had granted permission for the flights, and that the protesters were a violent mob behaving illegally. Certainly, the veal trade was a lucrative business. Bradshaw recalls that Barrett-Jolley was making about £500,000 a week when the flights were in full swing.

In an unrelated incident, Barrett-Jolley was later handed a lengthy prison sentence for smuggling £22 million worth of cocaine into the UK.

Chapter Thirty-Eight

Goodbye Coventry – Hello Birmingham

D an Mason was promoted to managing director of Coventry Newspapers in 1998. His first decision as MD was to appoint Alan Kirby editor of the *Evening Telegraph*, probably the last example of someone who joined a large regional newspaper as a junior reporter remaining with the company for life and finally being gifted the editorial chair.

It was becoming increasingly obvious to me by now that budget and staffing cuts as well as a new softer editorial approach towards the council were beginning to change the *Coventry Evening Telegraph* and that the newspaper no longer packed the punch it was once famous for. My first task in the morning was to sit down with the editor and deputy editor to go through page proofs of that day's paper with a view to choosing subjects for the leader column. But as the weeks and months passed it became more and more difficult to find any stories worthy of editorial comment. Many of the main items on a page, the 'page-leads', were by now so fluffy and lightweight and of a such a poor quality that they would hardly have merited a couple of paragraphs at the bottom of the page in the 1980s. Eventually, after I left, the daily leader column was scrapped bringing to an end the *Telegraph*'s reputation for fearless comment and finally drawing a line under the paper as it existed during the days of Geoff Elliott.

Dan Mason left Coventry in 1999 to become editor of the *Birmingham Post*. As his departure was announced Mason wrote to council chief executive Iain Roxburgh, a letter that revealed the extent of the council's growing influence on *Evening Telegraph* editorial policy under his editorship.

The letter from Mason to Roxburgh stated: "Although I immediately felt at home here, I recall that I needed a little gentle coaching. Do you remember those meetings between Brian Clack (Labour Coventry city council leader who died in office in 1993), you and me, following yet another 'council-bashing' story? Your patience at those times helped me enormously to form a balanced (I hope) view of what was justified and what was not, and inspired me to play a more supportive role in the city."

Needless to say, the person chiefly responsible for reporting the council's affairs and for writing most of the supposedly 'council-bashing' stories, that is to say me, was unaware of the 'gentle coaching' of the editor by the chief executive of Coventry city council, although it had become clear to me by the mid-1990s that the *Telegraph*'s combative approach to the council was no longer flavour of the month with the paper's executives. The letter from Mason to Roxburgh surprised me, but I suppose it ought not to have as there were plenty of signs of a new tougher approach by Coventry council to the media in general.

After the 1997 General Election Dan Mason persuaded me to switch jobs and become the *Evening Telegraph*'s chief feature writer, which he said would give me a wider field to write about. Quite clearly, this could have been interpreted as an attempt to address the council's concerns by removing me from the political front line and I've no doubt that's the way it was seen at the Council House. But any celebrations at Coventry council were premature as I spent much of the next three years writing feature articles criticising the council's shortcomings, effectively sidestepping Mason's strategy.

I'd formed a close professional and personal relationship with BBC Coventry and Warwickshire's new station controller Conal O'Donnell who took over in 1995 and we co-operated on many stories about the council, in particular the ongoing Coventry Contract Services scandal. Conal decided "to go for the council" in an attempt to boost CWR's poor listening figures, which he did. "Coventry council's conceit and general cack-handedness made critical journalism all too easy," he recalled.

It was clear, as the millennium approached, that the *Coventry Evening Telegraph* was beginning to be very wary of stories that were critical of the establishment, whether that was the police, the council or MPs, preferring instead to concentrate on fluffy soft articles and 'lifestyle' columns. A long investigation by a colleague into the alleged influence of Freemasons at Coventry's independent schools never saw the light of day following complaints to the editor from the schools. My weekly column became a source of friction when I wanted to write about the council's shortcomings and I began to feel I was in danger of fighting a losing battle.

Armed with the might of BBC WM's influential Ed Doolan mid-morning show from Birmingham, which he used as a battering ram against Coventry council, O'Donnell was beginning to make an impact and we became something of a double act, meeting regularly for lunch to plan tactics. He recently explained his thinking to me: "After reading your trenchant *Coventry Telegraph* pieces I decided to cultivate you as an ally even though I knew the *Coventry Telegraph* management hated CWR's guts.

"One of our earliest collaborations was to make sure Coventry council's accounts were inspected by our respective staffs for the first time in years. They didn't like it, especially as was inevitable quite a few little quirks were turned over.

"Doolan summoned the city treasurer to come onto the show over these accounts which he resisted and was daily mocked for his refusal until he gave in. After a while he became a fan of Doolan and saw we had a point over some of our inquiries."

The Coventry city treasurer, Peter Cordle, a gentle man and a committed Christian, was so upset over revelations about the financial irregularities of Coventry Contract Services that he announced his resignation live on the Ed Doolan programme, in verse for extra dramatic effect.

It became apparent that the Coventry council chief executive's attempts to persuade Dan Mason to tone down criticism of the local authority in the *Evening Telegraph* was not the only weapon in his armoury. O'Donnell began to feel the heat, as he recalls:

"Iain Roxburgh at first tried to charm us into co-operation. I stopped accepting his off the record briefings. I was summoned to his presence where he tried to persuade me to end our confrontational tone which he claimed was in any event against BBC guidelines. He had a copy of BBC guidelines on the table open at a supposedly relevant page as we spoke."

Things came to a head for O'Donnell in 1998. He was fronting a live recording of the city council election count when council workers decided in the early hours of the morning it was time to close the sports hall since all of the seats had been declared. However, CWR was still in the building and on-air, resulting in O'Donnell barricading the doors in a valiant attempt to carry on broadcasting. I referred to the incident in my *Evening Telegraph* column as "handbags at dawn".

This was followed by O'Donnell's revenge in which he spliced together extracts from Roxburgh interviews over several months to make the chief executive appear, at best, unhinged and took to broadcasting the tape with great glee. The lark was a clear breach of the BBC guidelines and the repercussions were brutal, as O'Donnell recalls: "Roxburgh went straight to the top – the BBC Director General no less – complaining that our coverage was actually harming the city. When he went to meetings trying to set up joint ventures with the private sector he claimed he felt mocked by the tone we set and sustained."

The BBC recalled O'Donnell to the Pebble Mill studios in Birmingham, putting paid to CWR's brief period of campaigning journalism, and I lost a brave and resourceful ally. Roxburgh, when he finally took early retirement in 2001, had served as Coventry council chief executive for 12 years, believed to be the longest period at the time for the head of any major local authority in Britain.

With Coventry having hardly recovered from the 1980s economic downturn, the recessions of the 1990s delivered a second bitter blow. Iconic 1950s landmarks symptomatic of Coventry's post-war reconstruction and optimism, including the Leofric Hotel and Owen Owen department store, went out of business, while the boarding-up of smaller shops became commonplace.

By the mid-1990s Coventry city council's regeneration efforts were in full swing. The council, typically, managed to recruit two chief officers to do one important job. City development director Duncan Sutherland and John McGuigan, director of economic development, were jointly responsible for reviving Coventry's economy, and as it happened both recognised the importance of keeping the local media onside.

Plans were hatched to flatten the area around Pool Meadow, including the former Hippodrome Theatre, a Coventry post-war icon much loved by *Evening Telegraph* readers who wrote to the paper in droves complaining about the 'destruction' of such a landmark. On top of this, there were plans to build new public squares leading up to the cathedral that were to be filled by bars, cafes and restaurants as well as apartments for 'city living'. The council also had its eyes on rebuilding huge swathes of the Sir Donald Gibson-designed shopping precinct.

Sutherland was always happy to brief me about his ideas but insisted we travel in his car outside of Coventry for lunch rather than risk him being spotted speaking to a journalist.

The *Coventry Telegraph*, by now well into its more positive relationship with the council, was naturally a big supporter of the Pool Meadow redevelopment and also backed demolition of the former Hippodrome, although most of the paper's readers were opposed and vented their anger via the letters page.

Regeneration had become something of an ugly word in Coventry by the mid-1990s. The council's attempts to breathe new life into the city centre a few years earlier proved controversial with construction of the Cathedral Lanes shopping centre and the placing of a huge big tent-like canopy over Broadgate, the historic heart of the city centre. Cathedral Lanes had been billed as a collection of high-end independent shops, but an economic downturn just as the scheme was completed meant that only the bigger high street names could afford the rents being demanded. As it turned out, there was nothing unique about Cathedral Lanes, and most people thought the Broadgate canopy was an absurd affectation.

Messing with Broadgate, which with the Cathedral took the full blast of the 1940 Blitz, proved to be a serious error of judgment by the council. There were huge protests from the Coventry public and conservationists, but the Pool Meadow and Broadgate schemes went ahead as planned. Complaints about the canopy featured regularly in the *Evening Telegraph* letters page way into the 1990s and beyond. In 2008, the council finally bowed to public opinion and had the Broadgate canopy removed.

In 2018, as if to underline a continuing battle between the council, whose instinct was to knock down 'outdated' buildings, and conservationists who wanted to preserve the best parts of Coventry's post-war redevelopment, the Government's conservation watchdog Historic England moved to impose Grade II listings on several of the city's 1950s landmarks including the former Hotel Leofric, the Locarno Dancehall (now the Central Library), the former Woolworth's building as well as the former British Home Stores and Marks and Spencer buildings. Historic England's decision prompted a predictably angry council response with the cabinet member for regeneration and jobs claiming the listing would act "as a disincentive to developers to go-ahead with long-awaited plans to rejuvenate the flagging central shopping area".

Historic England responded to the council's criticism with a clear statement of intent: "These newly listed buildings form part of the first, and among the largest, post-war city centre developments to be planned in the country.

"The innovative scheme for the precinct includes the earliest example of a shopping centre in England that separated cars and people, with a confident, kind and imaginative approach to public spaces for everyone.

"Coventry is a designated Heritage Action Zone and has also been named UK City of Culture 2021.

"The city's heritage and rare architecture have an important role to play in celebrating what is special about Coventry and in helping to bring about economic prosperity for those who live and work there."

By 1999, I realised the future for opinionated political writers in Coventry was not looking great. Rationalisation in the editorial department was in full swing and I'd spent two or three years fighting to justify continuing to attend the party conferences, the cost of which had caught the eye of the accountants now running the *CET* and the Birmingham papers. Dan Mason wanted me to justify my trips to the conferences, I said it was a matter for him as editor and he would have to decide.

It was suggested to me that I could continue to go to the conferences if I stayed in cheap, basic bed and breakfast accommodation rather than hotels – an offer I politely rejected. In fact, I told Mason I wasn't prepared to stay in accommodation for business trips which was of a lower standard than my own home. The editor gave in and I continued to attend the conferences on my terms.

In the summer of 2000, Dan Mason, who had been appointed editor of *The Birmingham Post*, asked me to join him and I duly became the *Post*'s chief reporter and subsequently public affairs editor focusing primarily on Britain's largest local authority, Birmingham city council. My long battle with Coventry council was over and, sadly, it was a relief to move on.

It was evident by then that efforts to get the Evening Telegraph circulation back to the prized 100,000-mark were over-ambitious. The long downward slide for regional newspapers was in full swing and the *CET* would do well to consolidate sales at 50,000.

Some of us were beginning to suspect that the internet would change for ever the way most people would access information in the future. But as ever in the world of newspapers, change was slow to come and openly resisted in some quarters. At the start of the 2000s the *CET* formed a New Media department to investigate ways of exploiting the opportunities offered by the internet, but this simply gave a new lease of life to reactionaries who 20 years before had resisted the change from typewriters to word processors. Editor Alan Kirby famously declared he wouldn't put the company's website address under the *Coventry Telegraph* masthead on the front page as "this internet thing will never take off".

Shortly before I left, management decided to invite a cross-section of *Evening Telegraph* readers to an early-evening reception with the aim of asking them what could be done to improve the paper and boost sales. Some 100 turned up, were given wine and canapes in order to relax them, then split into groups and sat around tables to be asked questions such as "what do you like about the *Telegraph*?", "what don't you like?", "what would you like to see in the paper that isn't there at the moment?", "which of the columnists do you like, or dislike?".

Unfortunately, pretty much everyone in the room turned out to be so loyal to the *Coventry Telegraph* that they couldn't think of any way in which the paper could be improved. All of the columnists were brilliant, everything was fantastic. And so, off into the night went 100 satisfied and slightly sozzled readers. It would have been more instructive, of course, to have selected 100 participants that did not read the *Evening Telegraph* and try to find out what would persuade them to do so, but no one thought of that.

Coventry, for once, managed to pull the stops out for the millennium celebrations by arranging for a spectacular tight-rope walk between the spires of Holy Trinity Church and the old cathedral. Frenchman Ramon Kelvink successfully completed the walk, watched by thousands gathered in Broadgate, and the event was screened live by the BBC. The death-defying stunt was the idea of Coventry and Warwickshire Promotions, an offshoot of the City Centre Company, an arms-length city council outfit designed to bring private sector thinking into regenerating the centre of Coventry.

It wasn't the first time such an event had been proposed. In 1884 when French tightrope walker Charles Blondin wanted to perform a similar feat, Coventry council refused permission. This time the council and the church authorities gave approval, but insisted Kelvink used a safety net.

Towards the end of 1999, with the millennium approaching, the *Coventry Evening Telegraph* began to consider what it could do to mark 1,000 years of history. Staff were asked to come up with ideas and I wrote to the managing director, Mike Hutchby, suggesting the paper work with the council to plant 1,000 trees across the city centre. Hutchby called me into his office and asked: "Where are these trees going to come from?" I explained that the paper would have to buy them. "Ah, right", Hutchby replied. And that was the last anyone ever heard of that idea.

Chapter Thirty-Nine

Stop Press

"The bank – the monster has to have its profits all the time. It can't wait. It'll die. No, taxes go on. When the monster stops growing, it dies. It can't stay one size." John Steinbeck, The Grapes of Wrath.

I walked out of the *Coventry Evening Telegraph* offices for the last time and couldn't help reflecting that the pace of change since 1986 had been extraordinary – some good, some not so good.

My first days at the *CET* coincided with the end of typewriters, and that meant, thank goodness, there was no longer any need to change typewriter ribbons, a skill I never could quite master. Word processors appeared and then personal computers and laptops, with a new frustration as the primitive kit seemed to spend quite a lot of time 'going down' with the consequent loss of written work and much cursing and fist waving by journalists at blank screens.

Pretty much all of the *CET*'s district offices had closed as part of relentless cost-cutting, the paper was down to just two editions a day, the canteen was no more and the golf society nothing but a fond memory of more enjoyable and relaxed times.

But even bigger changes to newspaper life were only just beginning. In 2006, the *CET* became a morning newspaper and dropped 'Evening' from its title. The switch, copied by many other evening newspapers across the country, allowed publishers to save money by getting rid of fleets of delivery vans and their drivers since their newspapers could be distributed by 'piggy-backing' on to national newspaper deliveries.

Newspaper management tried to spin the change as positive, claiming the switch to a morning paper enabled a new emphasis with the printed edition concentrating on exclusive and community news, leaving breaking news to its website. The reality, whichever way you look at it, was that the diminishing number of punters buying the printed version of the *Coventry Telegraph* were no longer getting the up to date news they once enjoyed and were steered instead to websites provided by Reach plc, the new name for Trinity Mirror, which are all called 'Live' as in *Coventry Live* and *Birmingham Live*, presumably in an effort to remind readers they are being fed news as it happens.

Ten years after I left, the *CET* moved out of its historic Corporation Street headquarters to smaller and cheaper offices on the other side of the ring road at the Coventry Canal Basin. Years of job cuts had taken their toll and the newspapers were now being printed at The Fort, a new Trinity Mirror printing works in Birmingham. The sprawling offices which used to house an editorial floor, separate advertising, promotions and accounts sections as well as a print room was simply too big and too expensive for requirements.

The Covid-19 pandemic generated ideal conditions to deliver ever more radical changes in the media world. The circulation of most printed newspapers fell at an even faster rate, but on the plus side newspaper websites were busier than ever with customers desperate to seek information on the worst health crisis for a generation. The events of an extraordinary year proved once and for all that newspapers could easily be produced by staff working from home, and as a result Reach plc announced it would close all but 15 of its UK offices, leaving most of its regional titles without bases in the areas they serve.

Reach says it intends to maintain hub offices in Belfast, Bristol, Birmingham, Dublin, Cardiff, Glasgow, Newcastle, Hull, Leeds, Liverpool, London, Greater Manchester, Nottingham, Plymouth and an office in the South-East of England. Daily titles including the *Cambridge News*, *Leicester Mercury* and *The Sentinel* in Stoke-on-Trent will no longer have an office on their patch.

A newspaper not having an office, or even several offices, in the town or area it serves would have been unthinkable even a few years ago, and it is the case that such premises have been a vital cornerstone of towns and communities for 150 years or more. It could be argued of course that Reach's decision to do away with most of its offices is simply an inevitable consequence of switching from printed newspapers to website newspapers, which can be written and designed from a front room, a coffee bar, or indeed anywhere in the world where there is access to the internet.

If video killed the radio star, did new technology see off local newspapers? The answer to that question is not really as straightforward as it may seem. The truth is that high circulation regional and city newspapers, those selling more than 100,000 a day, were already in decline 30 years ago when the internet was nothing more than a geeky fad. The long steady fall in newspaper sales which began at the end of the 1950s was always likely to accelerate as a result of societal change more than anything else. People had more money, more leisure time and were more outward looking because they travelled much more outside of the towns and cities where they lived. Television became an important factor in their lives and although it took a long time for newspaper managements to wake up and smell the coffee, more and more families, particularly the younger generation, were no longer interested in sitting down in the evening and reading the local newspaper. Employment patterns changed too with the disappearance of high-volume manufacturing, putting paid to workers passing time on the bus journey home by reading a copy of the local rag. Nor were newspapers any longer the sole source of advertising, with the internet providing a fast, viable alternative medium for people wishing to sell or buy cars and houses.

Another significant change which began in the 1970s and gathered pace in the 1980s and 1990s saw hundreds of independently owned newspapers and small local media groups swallowed up by vast and largely anonymous public limited companies. Reach plc, for example, publishes 240 regional newspapers as well as the *Daily Mirror, Sunday Mirror, The People, Daily Express, Sunday Express* and the *Daily Star*. These giants had one overriding aim – to maximise profits and pay dividends to their shareholders, although corporate greed might be a more apt description.

Newspapers that had jogged along quite happily for years making a decent amount of money for their owners were suddenly ordered to return profits that were impossible to achieve without wholesale budget cuts. Across the country, editors and executives sat hunched in their newsrooms staring glumly at spreadsheets trying to work out how on earth they could balance the books, but it didn't take long to realise the only way to do so was to put a great many people out of work.

The dreaded words 'economies of scale' became everyday currency as district editions and offices were shut down in order to save money, and newspapers which had once boasted of offering jobs for life were hit by round after round of redundancies. Where readers living in a small town once enjoyed several editions a day of their own local paper, they suddenly had to put up with perhaps a front page and one or two inside pages of local news in a product devoted almost entirely to events taking place in another much larger town or city down the road of which they had no interest.

Unsurprisingly, readers felt they were being taken for a ride and stopped buying such an inferior product and circulation fell even further resulting in district editions and newspapers being deemed unprofitable and closed for good.

The fact is it took a surprisingly long time for the internet to have any great impact on the way newspapers are produced. Resistant to change as ever, companies clung on doggedly to the belief, against all evidence, that print could still somehow have a bright future even though it was becoming difficult by the mid-2000s to see how this could possibly be the case. Trinity Mirror's early attempts to impose a 'digital first' regime at all of its regional newspapers, where the best stories would be first placed on websites before appearing in printed newspapers, failed initially because executives did not really have faith in the idea. Nor could they work out how websites could be 'monetised', that is make a profit and pay for themselves. This of course is an issue to which there are no clear answers even now.

The crushing juggernaut of the internet did of course prevail in the end, changing for ever the way that news is disseminated instantaneously across the world. And as I look back fondly now at the start of my career in 1975 under the tutelage of eccentric sub editors at the *Reading Chronicle and Berkshire Mercury*, it seems the way we were then is as remote from today as hansom cabs and quill pens. Was it a life worth living? Certainly. And undoubtedly better than working.